Bringing a Garden to Life

The Wiggly Wigglers Guide to bringing your Garden to Life

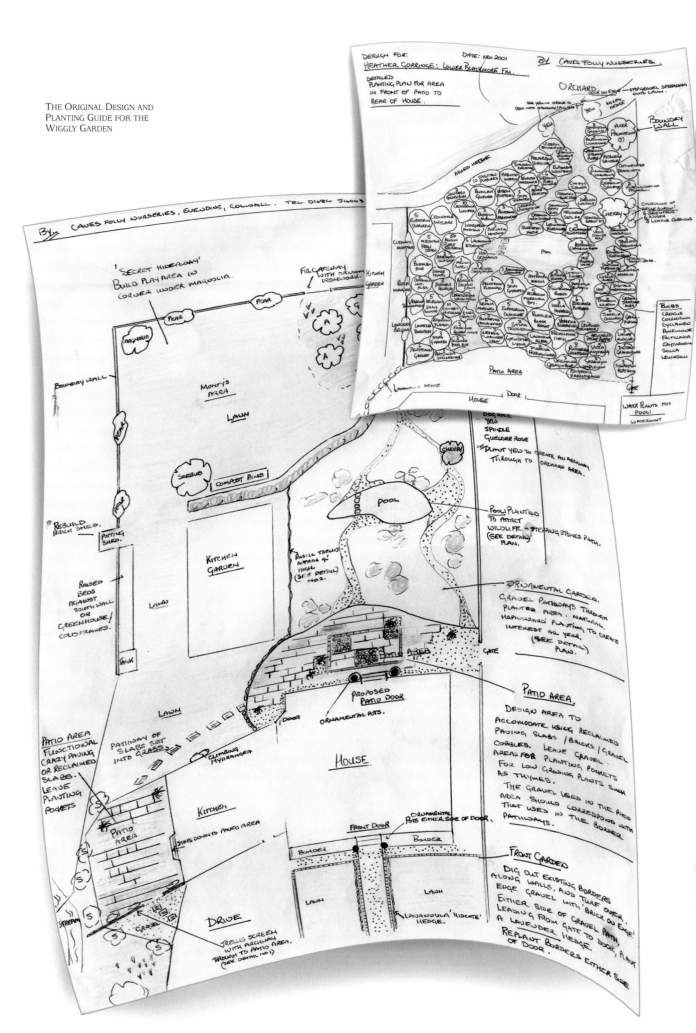

THE ORIGINAL DESIGN AND
PLANTING GUIDE FOR THE
WIGGLY GARDEN

Bringing a Garden to Life

The Wiggly Wigglers Guide to bringing your Garden to Life

by
Jenny Steel

Wiggly Wigglers

Published by:

Wiggly Wigglers
Lower Blakemere Farm,
Blakemere,
Hereford HR2 9PX.
Telephone: 01981 500391
www.wigglywigglers.co.uk

Book Copyright © 2006:

Wiggly Wigglers

Text Copyright © 2006:

Jenny Steel

Images Copyright © 2006:

Each of the photographs appearing
in this book is copyrighted in the
name of its individual photographer.

Designed, typeset and produced by:

Myst Ltd.
Whitehill Park,
Weobley,
Hereford HR4 8QT.
Telephone: 01544 318800

Printed by:

Scotprint
Gateside Commerce Park,
Haddington,
East Lothian EH41 3ST.
Telephone: 01620 828800

ISBN 10:   0-9553016-0-2
ISBN: 978-0-9553016-0-5

Photographed by Michael S Maloney (Myst Ltd) except:

Jenny Steel: Peacock Butterfly page 15; Nectar Garden page 19; Teasel with Hoverflies & Teasel Reservoir page 20; Whitetailed Bumblebee on Winter Aconite page 27; Dandelions pages 30–31; Newts page 36; Hazel Catkins page 49, Comma Butterfly on Pear page 49; Spindle Flowers page 53; Birch Images pages 54–55; Hazel Nuts page 57; Elderberries page 57; Field Maple page 58; Privet page 58; Yew page 58; Caterpillars page 60–61; Beech in Snow page 60; Beech Mast page 61; Blackthorn Sloes page 61; Dogwood page 61; Brimstone Egg page 61; Bird's Foot Trefoil Patch page 70; Greater Knapweed page 74; Cornflower page 76; Cornfields page 77; Hoverfly on Dahlia page 82; Black Hoverfly page 83; Meadow Brown Butterfly page 87; Mint Leaf Beetles page 97; Ladybirds page 98; Solitary Bees page 109; Log Pile page 113; Sunflower page 114; Pollen Beetles page 115; Mole page 122; Lavender page 126–127; Agrimony page 132; Flowering Rush page 135; Greater Knapweed page 136; Greater Spearwort page 136; Lady's Bedstraw page 138; Marsh Woundwort page 140; Meadow Saxifrage page 141; Sheepsbit Scabious page 143; Small Scabious page 144; St. John's Wort page 146; Wild Strawberry page 148; Yellow Loosestrife page 149;

John Harding: Barn Owl page 16; Goldfinches page 21 & 31; Collecting Mud page 39; Purple Loosestrife (inset) 41; Song Thrushes pages 50–51; Blackthorn page 56; Brambling page 59; Tits page 98; House Sparrow page 106; Greenfinch page 115; Greater Spotted Woodpecker page 116; Feeding Robins page 116; Blue Tits page 117; Nuthatch page 117;

Mark Eccleston: Frosted Teasel page 21; Robin page 22; Bee on Catkin page 27; Southern Hawker Dragonfly page 34; Toads page 38; Frogs page 42; Common Blue Damselfly page 43; Broad Bodied Chaser page 43; Spindle Seedpods pages 52–53; Common Blue Butterfly pages 66–67; Brimstone Butterfly page 69; Yellow Hoverfly page 83; Solitary Bee page 86; Orange Tip Butterfly page 86; Red Admiral Butterfly page 87; Rhubarb page 99; Green Veined White Butterfly page 121; Green Lacewing page 121; Cardinal Beetle page 121; Hemp Agrimony page 137; Soft Rush page 145; Wood Anemone page 149;

Rachel Jones: Garden Construction pages 24–25 & 28–29; Farmer Phil with Mole page 122;

Robert Lee: Marsh Bedstraw page 139; Marsh Cinquefoil page 140; Skullcap page 144;

John Gardner: Hedgehog page 98.

Contents

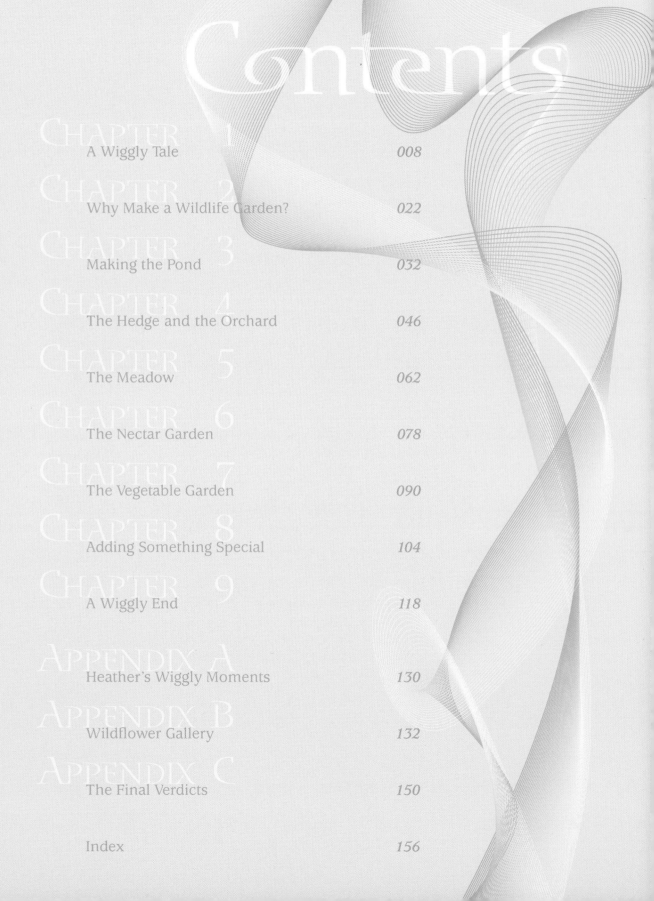

Jenny's Introduction

I first came across Wiggly Wigglers in the early 1990s. Just as they were establishing their new business, I was setting up a nursery growing plants especially for wildlife gardeners—wild-flowers and shrubs, cottage garden plants and herbs with nectar and pollen for insects. We had a common vision: to educate gardeners in the ways of gardening naturally and sustainably, taking account of the environment and encouraging wildlife. It was inevitable that our paths would cross many times over the next ten years, and in 2003 I visited their new wild-life garden, which was just one year old. I was completely bowled over. It was exactly the sort of wildlife garden that I had been promoting in my own work—not a wild unkempt mess but vibrant, colourful and absolutely brimming with life. This book is about that garden, its construction and wildlife but it also shows you how to create a wildlife garden of your own, using Wiggly Wigglers' ideas and principles.

Everyone at Wiggly Wigglers and Lower Blakemere Farm has played a part in this book, generously offering their encouragement and enthusiasm as well as their thoughts and comments about the garden and its wildlife. I would like to thank every one of them, but especially Heather. Without her amazing energy, positivity and passion, this book, and I suspect this garden, would never have happened.

Jenny Steel

Heather's Introduction

For years the easy option was to blame farmers for well… just about everything that was wrong with our natural environment. 'There aren't as many goldfinches around—that'll be the farmers!' 'All the hedges have disappeared—that'll be the farmers!' And yet what have we as gardeners been up to over the past thirty years or so? Well, we have certainly concentrated on a smooth stripy lawn, which we have watered and sprayed with chemicals that have long been banned in the agricultural world. We've planted up our double begonias, which may look wonderful but provide no nectar for bugs and butterflies. And then how do we sort out our boundaries with our neighbours? No wildlife friendly hedge—just a larch lap fence that we paint in some trendy new colour—Barley Blue was just so 90's wasn't it? Then we moan about how long it takes us to tend our plot—endless mowing, spraying and weeding! Oh, and the organic argument? Well, once again if we compare a garden to a farm, farmers face massive difficulties to get organic status—all the while trying to deal with hundreds of acres—whereas you and I just have to stop spraying and look for alternative gardening methods that could never be cost effective for a farmer.

Developing our own 'Natural Garden' here has taught me that not only does it demonstrate a fantastic contribution that we can all easily make to our wider environment, but it also looks wonderful and is actually much easier to tend than a conventional garden. Gardening 'The Wiggly Way' has really brought our garden to life. Hopefully this book will give you the courage to try it too.

Heather Gorringe

Chapter 1

A Wiggly Tale

Imagine an idyllic rural setting—rolling hills clothed with green oak trees, gently sloping fields full of wheat and contented cows, no noise except for the twitter of a swallow and the buzz of a bumblebee. Butterflies flit from wildflower to wildflower along the hedgerows in the evening sunlight, and as dusk approaches the ghostly outline of a barn owl quarters the fields, searching for voles and mice to take to her growing brood in a hole in a nearby tree.

You could be forgiven for imagining that this was England perhaps fifty or sixty years ago, or maybe even longer. But this scene is now and this is Lower Blakemere Farm on the very edge of Herefordshire, a thriving mixed farm with an unexpected heart at its centre. It is the home of Wiggly Wigglers, the successful organic gardening company that has caught the imagination of a new legion of gardeners—people who want to get the best from their gardens without compromising the environment. Wiggly Wigglers has managed to capture in their approach the essence of what so many people now wish to bring to their gardens or allotments—a sense that they are gardening in tune with nature.

And here on the farm, where wildlife lives in harmony with the raising of cattle and the growing of crops, is another surprise. Close to the farm buildings where the fifteen or so people who make up the Wiggly Wigglers team spend their busy days answering telephones and packing parcels, a stunning wildlife garden has been created to reinforce the staff's commitment to their principles. A garden with a wildflower meadow, a wildlife pond, large areas of nectar plants to tempt the bumblebees from the farmland, and a vegetable plot, overflowing with healthy rows of root crops, salad leaves and all

manner of good things to eat. And not surprisingly the foundations of this garden are the organic principles that everyone here holds so dear.

This book is about the making of that garden and the wildlife that visits it. But this isn't just the story of a beautiful garden deep in the countryside, with no relevance to a tiny suburban plot, or a window box hanging onto the side of a tower block in the middle of a city. Everything about this garden is relevant to your garden if you want to create something brimming with life. It's about creating an area that is in harmony with its surroundings, where nature is taken into account and nurtured, where every decision made has a single thought behind it. Will this benefit the immediate environment and the wildlife round about? And if some of the damage we have done to our environment in the last fifty years is repaired with this approach, so much the better.

Anyone with a garden, or access to even a tiny slice of outdoor space, can learn from the Wiggly Wigglers approach to gardening. Read this book, bring your garden to life, and you and your immediate environment could be all the better for it.

How it all began

Wiggly Wigglers began life in 1990 with a vision for the future. Heather Gorringe, a forward thinking, energetic young woman had an ambition—to create a business that would unite, and become an integral part of, her local community in the place where she had spent her whole life so far—West Herefordshire. With a few pounds and an innovative idea she set out to earn herself a living, but in spite of her foresight, she had little idea of just how successful her company would eventually become.

The long term ideals of Wiggly Wigglers were set even then—to create employment for local people, source products locally and make sure that all aspects of the business were environmentally sustainable.

THE VIEW FROM MONTY'S BEDROOM WINDOW:
THE WIGGLY GARDEN HIBERNATES,
WINTER 2005

Heather believed from the very start that we can all make a positive and measurable impact on our surroundings by changing the way that we maintain our gardens. She set out with a commitment to organic principles and sustainable living, and over time her ideals came to include the nurturing of local wildlife.

Through sheer hard work and drive, Heather established the basis of the present company by composting locally available materials using worms, the 'Wigglers' of her company's name. Worm composting was popular in America but had yet to be accepted as common practice in gardens in the UK. As the worms multiplied they were supplied to organic gardening businesses for composting kits as this method of recycling garden and kitchen waste slowly began to take off. Demand for her product grew, and it rapidly became obvious to Heather that she needed to connect directly with the growing numbers of organic gardeners out there, who shared her belief that every garden could be managed in a way that made it environmentally stable as well as a great habitat for wildlife.

Three years after Wiggly Wigglers was born, Heather moved her office to Lower Blakemere Farm, the family home she shares with her husband Phil and son Monty, initially using a bedroom as an office. From here the mail order side of the business was born, together with a website, and it was not long before a handful of staff, all local, were helping to develop and market the range of organic gardening products for which the company is now famous, as well as the composting kits they originally produced. Wildflower seeds and plants and wildlife gardening products have followed with great success, as more and more gardeners shun the chemical ways of the last few decades. It was not long before farm buildings were converted into offices and despatch areas, and what was initially a great idea became a thriving business employing fourteen staff members and spawning several local businesses eager to supply Wigglies with locally made items such as bird boxes and insect homes.

In 2002 the concept of the wildlife garden came to life as a place where products could be trialed and photographed, staff could relax and wildlife could thrive and shelter, a place where life on the farm and the business would come together.

Feature Creature

Barn Owl

One of the most exciting animals on Lower Blakemere Farm is the barn owl. These pale, almost ghostly birds are best viewed at dusk and have been seen on the farm many times. Sadly they have declined dramatically throughout Britain in the last fifty years due to the loss of nest sites and prey, and there are now only 4–5,000 breeding pairs remaining. This beautiful bird faces a number of hazards in our rural environment and many die as a result of colliding with traffic on busy roads. Countless old farm buildings have been converted to dwellings, depriving the owls of good nest sites. In captivity they may live to reach twenty years, but in the dangerous countryside, few live beyond five years old.

The barn owl relies mainly on small mammals for its food, especially the short tailed field vole, and hunts at dusk on silent wings. It does this by 'quartering' a grassy field or meadow—flying slowly up and down, covering the whole area thoroughly and checking the ground for small movements and sounds. The barn owl has fantastic hearing and can detect the rustle of a vole in the grass from several metres away. Its white heart-shaped facial disc helps to funnel sounds to the ears, which are situated asymmetrically on either side of the head near the eyes. After digesting a meal, the owl produces a pellet of bones and fur, the contents of which can tell us a great deal about its diet.

Profile of Heather

Heather began her career by studying design, but life in the heart of the Herefordshire countryside opened her eyes to the decline of local communities—something she desperately wanted to do something about.

Working initially for her father, driving tractors and working on the land imbued her with an independence, strength of character and a 'can-do' attitude which meant that putting together her own business was a logical step that held no fears for her. She continues to be passionate about community and her drive and sense of humour have taken Wiggly Wigglers from strength to strength, creating local jobs and involving local people on open days. Winning awards for her business is something she regularly takes in her stride.

Lower Blakemere Farm

Heather's approach to her business revolves strongly around the concept of links—between members of her community, between small local businesses and especially between the surrounding countryside and the garden. Unlike the business, the farm itself, under the care of Phil, Heather's husband, is not run on organic principles but great care is taken to farm in tune with the environment. Pesticide use is carefully planned on the farm, as Phil knows the value of encouraging beneficial insects and other wildlife, which often do a better job than any chemicals can. Dead wood is left wherever it is feasible, not only to create homes for the two resident pairs of barn owls on the farm, but also to enable populations of beetles and other wood devouring creatures to build up. These in turn provide food for many of the small mammals and birds around the farmland, creatures that earn their keep by naturally and safely removing unwanted pests.

There is plenty of other wildlife on the farm including hares, two species of deer, bats and a great variety of bird life. A pond in the farmyard supports a population of the nationally rare and protected great crested newt, and coots and moorhens have also made their homes here.

But the surrounding farmland isn't simply another habitat for the wildlife that the Wiggly team are trying to encourage. It is also an integral part of the company, as Phil grows some of the seed varieties that find their way into the bird food mixes sold by mail order. Farm equipment is now used to clean and mix the blends that are carefully chosen to appeal to a variety of bird species. Farm and business are closely linked.

Making an Organic Statement

Organic gardening means different things to different people, but the crucial concept is that you are gardening in harmony with nature. If you garden organically you turn your back on artificial fertilisers and feed the soil with compost. Healthy soil means healthy plants, which are more able to resist disease. You put away chemical pesticides and allow nature to deal with infestations of aphids or slugs. These creatures, which as gardeners we may prefer not to have around in our gardens, provide food for other wildlife such as bluetits, hedgehogs or song thrushes, and the more of these beneficial creatures you have in your garden, the fewer problems you will get from pests and diseases. Organic gardening and wildlife gardening go hand in hand. One cannot work without the other.

TOP: EARLY DAYS IN THE NECTAR GARDEN
BOTTOM: THE EVER CHANGING MEADOW, AUGUST 2002

If you garden organically you will straight away find that you have more wildlife around. Also your local wildlife can work for you, keeping pest species in check and creating a balance in the garden, where no one creature becomes dominant and causes problems. Once you stop using chemicals a harmonious, natural balance evolves, and of course you will automatically have more bees, ladybirds and butterflies, because pesticides kill the 'nice' insects as well as the 'nasty' ones.

You can also help nature by using companion planting, which is an important element of gardening organically. This involves deliberately encouraging beneficial insects such as hoverflies and ladybirds to vulnerable plants. Both hoverflies and ladybirds feed on aphids, so encouraging these insects to broad beans may well keep the blackfly under control. Another aspect of companion planting involves placing certain compatible plants together. Onions for example, planted close to carrots, will disguise their distinctive carroty smell, which attracts the carrot root fly. Organic gardening is all about using nature to your advantage, looking after your soil by composting organic waste and making full use of the natural relationships within the garden ecosystem.

Teasel

Focal Flower

The teasel has to be one of the best wildlife plants to add to any garden because its flowers and seeds attract so many different creatures. In summer the heads of tiny pink blossoms have both nectar and pollen which means that many types of bees, hoverflies, even beetles (some species live entirely on pollen) spend a great deal of time crawling over its lovely spiky flower heads. As summer draws to a close, the large seeds ripen, providing a great source of food for goldfinches. These almost tropically coloured birds seek out the teasel heads and spend long periods of time carefully extracting the seeds with their beaks. As a single teasel can produce ten or more heads and each head over a hundred seeds, this is a very important food source and keeps the finches coming back to your garden.

In the past teasel heads were used for 'teasing' wool, combing out the debris and straightening the fibres, thus making the wool easier to spin. They were also used to raise the pile on cloth after it had been woven. A special variety known as fuller's teasel (a fuller being someone who cleaned cloth after weaving) was employed especially for this purpose as it has even spikier heads making it a more effective tool. Teasels were thought to have other very special properties. The huge leaves clasp the stalk, where they make a basin or reservoir where rainwater collects. This was known as the Bath of Venus and the water in it was thought to cure eye infections and also get rid of freckles! Small birds often drink from this convenient water supply, making the teasel an even more useful wildlife plant.

Chapter **2**

Why make a Wildlife Garden?

The staff at Wiggly Wigglers decided to make a wildlife garden at their headquarters for a number of reasons. First and foremost they wanted somewhere for customers and friends to see what the company was all about and to demonstrate that they practised what they preached. The intention was to have Open Days to raise money for charity, when people could visit, admire the garden and find out more about what went on there. Convincing visitors that wildlife gardens are not overgrown jungles but beautiful places, thoughtfully planned and planted, was a primary objective hopefully changing the way they thought about their own plots. Showing visitors the wonderful new garden was to be instrumental in inspiring them.

Secondly, it was important to have a space where any new product, such as a bird feeder or compost bin could be tried out, so that they knew for certain that it did what it was supposed to do. Then of course in the Wiggly spirit of keeping things local, somewhere to photograph the products from the catalogue was essential. And like so many people involved in gardening they wanted, quite simply, to provide a space that could be enjoyed by everyone in quiet moments, with nature all around to motivate them and keep them on their toes.

The new garden fulfilled all of these things—in good weather the staff hold meetings outside amongst the wildlife and plants. And who can blame them? Why sit inside when you can enjoy what you have created and be inspired by it? But there was however, yet another reason for creating this wonderful space. There is nothing like a visit from royalty to galvanize thoughts and actions, and when that visitor is Prince Charles, things start to happen! As Lower Blakemere Farm is part of the Duchy of Cornwall, the Prince had

been an occasional visitor. This time, a meeting of Duchy tenants was to be held at the farm, so it was important to ensure that the bulk of the garden was finished before his arrival at the beginning of May 2002. No one wanted HRH, whose thoughts about gardening and the environment were legendary, to be gazing from the dining room onto a large patch of mud and concrete! It was all hands on deck to get something done before he arrived.

However hastily the work was to be done, it was important that the area reflected everyone's ideas about how this special garden should look—after all it was to be something that the team would see on a daily basis, so it had to look beautiful as well as being attractive to wildlife. Everyone at Wiggly Wigglers at that time was involved in the discussions about how the garden should be and they pooled their thoughts and suggestions. Starting with the premise that every garden can be a great wildlife habitat and an important part of the wider environment, they definitely knew what they didn't want—including expanses of boring lawn, rows of bedding plants or useless flowering plants with no nectar or pollen to attract insects.

What they did want was a garden that included each of the habitats that are known to be good for wildlife. As big a pond as there was room for was essential, to bring newts, frogs and dragonflies right into the heart of the area. The pond was also to be somewhere that birds could bathe in safety and the local hedgehogs could find a drink. They wanted a meadow overflowing with wildflowers to entice plenty of butterflies and other insects from the countryside round about. A hedge of native spiky shrubs with lots of berries to encourage local birds to feed and build their nests was also an important feature and, somewhere in the garden, a sea of spring and summer nectar plants with colours to take the breath away. Lastly the team planned to plant a good variety of wild-flowers—as many different types as there was room for—in every spare nook and cranny, weaving a tapestry of vitally important species that would hold everything else together.

Clearly it was important that this special garden was professionally designed from the start, so Bridget Evans of Caves Folly Nurseries, a leading organic garden designer and RHS medal winner, was commissioned to help out. She incorporated all the habitats required for the garden into her plans and made suggestions for good wildlife-attracting plants. After consultation, discussion and a few changes, work began early in 2002 to transform the area around Lower Blakemere Farmhouse. What had largely been an expanse of concrete and grass was to be transformed, with lots of hard work, into the wonderful garden that is now admired by everyone on a daily basis. Little did the Wiggly staff imagine that within just one year there would be dragonflies and red admirals, great crested newts and hedgehogs, happily at home in this brand new garden.

Bridget's design started with a nectar plant area close to the house, full of ornamental varieties mulched with stones. The planting here was haphazard, creating a sea of vegetation that visitors could walk amongst without stepping on the plants. This was a stroke of genius. It meant that it would be possible to get close to every plant, (something that it is difficult to do where plants are in a border), weave between them and examine every bee, butterfly and hoverfly at close quarters. In the middle of this area was to be the pond, surrounded by a mixture of native wetland wildflowers such as water mint, purple loosestrife, cotton grass, marsh marigold and water forget-me-not, plus a few non-natives to add colour and variety. The nectar area was to be separated from the raised beds of the vegetable garden by a hand made willow trellis fence, which was very much in keeping with the natural feel that was needed throughout the whole garden area.

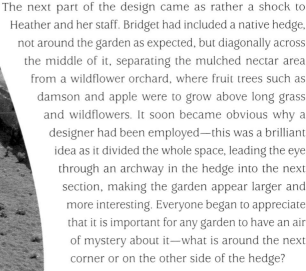

The next part of the design came as rather a shock to Heather and her staff. Bridget had included a native hedge, not around the garden as expected, but diagonally across the middle of it, separating the mulched nectar area from a wildflower orchard, where fruit trees such as damson and apple were to grow above long grass and wildflowers. It soon became obvious why a designer had been employed—this was a brilliant idea as it divided the whole space, leading the eye through an archway in the hedge into the next section, making the garden appear larger and more interesting. Everyone began to appreciate that it is important for any garden to have an air of mystery about it—what is around the next corner or on the other side of the hedge?

The hedge itself was to be composed of native shrubs such as hawthorn, dogwood, spindle and field maple, a wonderful mix of the kind of species that once lined our roadsides and lanes, providing food and shelter for wildlife, especially birds and small mammals. The archway area through to the meadow was to be planted with yew because of its ability to grow densely and respond well to clipping and shaping.

LEFT TOP: FARMER PHIL PUTS HIS BACK INTO IT
LEFT MIDDLE: HAVING THE RIGHT TOOLS FOR THE JOB
LEFT BOTTOM: SOME JOBS HAVE TO BE DONE BY HAND
RIGHT TOP: WILL IT EVER GROW?   MAY 2002
RIGHT MIDDLE: AT LAST, THE HARD WORK IS OVER
RIGHT BOTTOM: JODIE DIGGING OVER THE VEGETABLE BEDS

One asset in the existing garden was the old brick wall all around the boundary. This provided not just shelter for the plants and wildlife but places where many insects could find a home or small birds such as blue tits could search for holes to build their nests. Good use had been made of these walls in the past and some wonderful old pear trees grew against them in one area. Bridget had incorporated the walls into her design by including shade-loving plants in their shadows.

Even before the garden had started to take shape it was obvious that there were plenty of bumblebees around, making their homes in the wildlife friendly farmland all about and even, sometimes, in the boundary walls of the garden area. There was also plenty of nectar and pollen out there for them, something without which they cannot survive, although the plan for the garden made sure that an abundance of good bumblebee plants would be included. Bumblebees are quite adaptable insects and can be found in most habitats but it was important that the new garden catered for their every need.

Bumblebee

The bumblebee year begins in February or March when the first queen bees come out of hibernation into the weak, early spring sunshine. They are desperate for food after several months of living on their fat stores, so will investigate anything in flower. Favourite nectar sources early in the year are bulbs, hellebores and the odd dandelion that happens to open its petals. Any bumblebee around at this time will be a female queen that survived the winter. Last autumn she will have excavated a small hole in the soil, often in a north facing position, and spent the winter out of harm's way. The first sunny days will have warmed and woken her and, as well as searching for food, she will be seeking a nest site to lay her first eggs. If you see a bumblebee in early spring, spend a few minutes watching her. She will fly back and forth close to the ground, using her sense of smell to try and detect an old mouse nest. This is her preferred nest site, although she will make a nest of her own, perhaps in a hole in a stone wall or even in a compost heap, if she can't find a vacant mouse home. Here she will lay her eggs and feed the larvae with nectar and pollen. Three to four weeks later the young bumblebees will emerge from the nest. Depending on the species, this can be any time between April and June, but May is the usual month to see new small bumblebees in the garden.

There are about 24 species of bumblebee in the UK and only a few are relatively common: several are on the edge of extinction. Their numbers have declined by 60% since the 1970s due to the loss of their habitat. Fewer wildflowers has reduced the availability of pollen and nectar, but, thankfully, gardens can accommodate a range of plants that provide food for them, Species of medicks, clovers and trefoils, once common hay meadow plants, are favourites with many other insects as well as our furry friends. Bumblebees also love dead nettles, scabious, knapweed and Buddleia all of which were included in the garden.

This was to be a proper working garden, not a show garden where impractical planting or weird features made it difficult to maintain. Heather of course actually lives at Lower Blakemere Farm with her husband Phil and young son Monty. Monty needed somewhere to play, so a grassy area where he could kick a football about with his friends was a necessity. This part of the garden was positioned next to the wildflower meadow behind the hedge, where footballs would not flatten flowers (hopefully) and the longer grass of the meadow gave informality to this corner.

A kitchen garden too was essential, not just for visitors to see the various composting methods Wiggly Wigglers use, but to allow those working here to occasionally find something to make lunch a little more tasty!

Overall the design of the garden satisfied all criteria. Lastly it was important that recycled materials were used as much as possible. Reclaimed paving was incorporated into a patio area close to the house and old railway sleepers were brought in to make the raised beds in the vegetable area.

The end product was a 'complete' garden, a design that included everything a garden should have— flowers, vegetables, water, trees, grassy places and sitting out areas. Everything Heather and her team had asked for—but also everything wildlife needed—was in this wonderful design.

With the plan approved everyone was anxious to get started. Time was limited and an important visitor was expected...

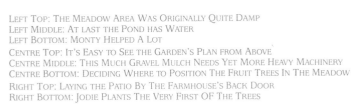

LEFT TOP: THE MEADOW AREA WAS ORIGINALLY QUITE DAMP
LEFT MIDDLE: AT LAST THE POND HAS WATER
LEFT BOTTOM: MONTY HELPED A LOT
CENTRE TOP: IT'S EASY TO SEE THE GARDEN'S PLAN FROM ABOVE
CENTRE MIDDLE: THIS MUCH GRAVEL MULCH NEEDS YET MORE HEAVY MACHINERY
CENTRE BOTTOM: DECIDING WHERE TO POSITION THE FRUIT TREES IN THE MEADOW
RIGHT TOP: LAYING THE PATIO BY THE FARMHOUSE'S BACK DOOR
RIGHT BOTTOM: JODIE PLANTS THE VERY FIRST OF THE TREES

The dandelion is a wildflower that occurs all around us, but is it really appreciated? In springtime this bright flower is one of the best early sources of nectar and pollen for butterflies and bumblebees, and these insects will often choose dandelions in preference to anything you may have thoughtfully planted in the garden for them. As well as sprinkling its golden flowers through your lawn, the dandelion has the ability to hang on tenaciously in the tiniest amount of soil, opening its petals on roadside verges and even in cracks in paving or walls. Its ability to survive in all conditions is mainly due to two important attributes. Firstly it has a long taproot that anchors it down, searching out moisture and nutrients. This taproot is also almost impossible to remove from the soil without leaving a bit behind (as all gardeners know) from

Dandelion

which the plant will grow again. Secondly it has a rosette of very flat leaves, enabling it to survive mowing or grazing by animals. In April the small tortoiseshell butterfly in particular seeks out this plant, but peacock butterflies, early bumblebees and honeybees too all appreciate the nectar and pollen that it provides. Once the seeds have set, goldfinches and greenfinches will argue over them.

Perhaps we should be celebrating the dandelion and appreciating its virtues. As well as its wildlife attracting abilities, it is edible and full of vitamins and minerals. In the past it was prized as a tonic, its new leaves cleansing the kidneys and earning it the dubious reputation as being a plant that caused bed-wetting, a little bit of folk-lore that still remains in our modern playgrounds. Its exceptional nutritional value is now recognised again and it is often available as a salad plant in supermarkets. In the Wiggly Garden dandelions are left in Monty's lawn to feed insects and finches.

chapter

3

Making the Pond

Once the initial preparation of the garden had been completed and the decisions about the boundaries of the different areas had been made, the exciting time came to dig out the pond. This habitat was to be the heart of the garden and everyone had very clear ideas about how they wanted it to look. Formal it was certainly not going to be! Instead, a natural looking pool was required so as to resemble the ponds that exist in the surrounding farmland. It was to have all the attributes of the perfect wildlife pond—lots of colourful native wildflowers around its margins, white water lilies in the deeper parts, masses of oxygenating weeds and some gently sloping edges where the local wildlife could reach the water in safety. It also needed to be close to other vegetation, where small frogs or newts could take refuge as they left the water in early summer.

It was important that the pond was not immediately visible to visitors entering the garden, so the surrounding planting was planned to visually shield it from other areas. It was to be an unexpected surprise—a little jewel amidst a sea of plants all buzzing with life. Heather imagined wandering into the garden on a bright summer's morning and coming across this small expanse of sparkling water with dragonflies buzzing around and frogs plopping into the shallows. This would mean that even those most familiar with the garden would still experience that element of astonishment every time the pond came into view.

The end of February was the starting date. This is actually a good time to create any new pond as it has the chance to accumulate a little rainwater before planting. After Heather outlined the shape she liked on the ground (using canes with string around them—a good way of judging whether the shape of a pond will sit well with the rest of the garden) Pip's father-in-law Ron took the driver's seat in the JCB and set to work—serious equipment was needed to help create this watery oasis. An elongated teardrop shape was excavated, with the shallower water at the narrow end. This design gave plenty of gently sloping edges where frogs, toads and hopefully newts could gain easy access to the water, and birds and hedgehogs could drink in safety. Great care was taken to make sure that the pond edges were level as this eliminated any unsightly pond liner showing.

Digging began on a cold morning and the unwanted soil was distributed around the garden, filling dips and holes. A deep area of about 1.5 metres was created at the wider end, from which the bottom shelved up to the shallower sides. The deep spot would provide a refuge for frogs in the winter—sometimes the males spend the colder weather deep in the mud at the bottom of a pond. This deeper place was also the best spot to plant water lilies. Once the shape was right, with a little adjustment from Ron and the JCB, the team stood back and admired their work—a big muddy hole! A lot of imagination was needed to envisage the summer ahead when this spot would be the garden's focal point.

The next task was to measure the area and order a pond liner. Butyl was chosen as this usually has a lifetime's guarantee, and the plan was that the pond should be around for many years to come. There is a useful formula to calculate the size of liner needed for any pond. Add twice the depth measurement to the width and the length of the hole, plus an extra metre for the overlap around the edges. While waiting for the liner to arrive the work continued. The bottom of the hole was carefully covered with a few inches of soft sand. This makes sure that the liner is protected from any sharp stones that may poke through and puncture it. On its arrival the liner was unfolded and gently manoeuvred into place, making sure that it overlapped the edges evenly all around. This is a tricky job, especially with a large liner, so everyone available

LEFT: 'MIRACLES TAKE A LITTLE LONGER…' A SOUTHERN HAWKER
DRAGONFLY EMERGES FROM ITS UNDERWATER LARVAL STAGE
CENTRE TOP: PIP SPREADS A LAYER OF SAND TO PROTECT THE LINER
CENTRE MIDDLE: BIG POND, HUGE LINER!
CENTRE BOTTOM: ADDING SOIL TO THE MARGINAL PLANTING SHELVES
RIGHT: WATER LILLY LEAVES SURFACE, NOW FOR SOME FLOWERS

helped, allowing the butyl to drape gently into the hole and folding any excess material around the edges before the next stage. In order to make the pond as natural looking as possible, the liner was covered with a ten centimetre layer of soil. The soil at Lower Blakemere is rather stony so several of the team spent some time sieving it by hand to remove anything sharp that could have damaged the liner. This was a long and laborious job, but was definitely worthwhile. The liner was then covered with this soft, stone-free soil, into which the wetland species were to be planted.

So the time had come to fill the pond with water. Fortunately the farm has a supply of sweet spring water (used for the cattle on the farm), which meant it was not necessary to use tap water, which can contain large amounts of chemicals. These can create an imbalance in the water causing blanket weed and other algae to proliferate. A hosepipe was used to fill the pond, running it gently onto a piece of matting to prevent the trickling water from disturbing the soil layer. After a day or two, when the water had settled, some of Phil's homegrown barley straw was added. This cleverly helps to prevent the build up of algae, which often happens when a new pond is created.

Heather recalls the relief she felt when the pond was finally dug out and filled with water. 'Having done all this hard work there was nothing for it but to cool off. It was shoes off and trousers up (for those of us who were brave enough) to get a frog's eye view of our new habitat! We knew that once there were plants and wildlife, we would never be able to have this experience again! Only Toast the dog was perhaps a little too enthusiastic. She rushed into the water and made a small hole in the liner with one of her claws. Thankfully it was close enough to the edge not to matter!'

The next task was to plant the wetland species. Back in 2002 Wiggly Wigglers did not grow their own pond plants, so when it came to planting they had to be content with the rather limited range of native species available then. In a wildlife pond, plants in planting baskets can look very artificial and the team wanted as natural a look as possible, so the plants were taken from their pots and their roots gently pushed in the soil covering the liner. This was a wet, muddy but important job. Plants such as marsh marigold, purple loosestrife, brooklime and ragged robin went around the edges in the shallow water.

Great crested newts are one of Britain's treasures—internationally they are rare and protected amphibians but in this country we are fortunate in having many breeding populations. In the wild they can be found in various habitats, but ponds on farmland seem to have the best conditions for them. They will readily use a garden pond if they are in your area, as long as it is quite large and deep and has some clear margins to allow the males to display to the females at breeding time. They prefer ponds with no frogs, toads or fish, although they will tolerate other newt species. However if a pond is large enough, several of these amphibian species can exist in harmony. A garden pond of a metre in depth containing plenty of vegetation could be an ideal place for them. The surrounding habitat is of importance too, as once they have bred, the adult newts leave the water to find shelter in areas of damp scrub, hedges and ditches. Dense shrubs and log piles close to your pond will provide the shelter they require.

Great Crested Newt

In spring the males, which may reach 15 centimetres in length, find their way to a suitable breeding pond. Great crested newts are almost black in colour, and in the springtime the males have wavy crests along their backs and bright orange patterned stomachs. Once in the water, they may remain there for as little as one month or as long as seven months, although the majority will have left the pond for the surrounding habitat by August. The female great crested newt can reach 18 centimetres in length. She lacks the male's impressive crest, but does have a colourful orange and black mottled stomach. After the male's tail-lashing display, the newts mate and the females lay their eggs singly on water plants, hiding each sticky egg by wrapping a plant leaf around it. The newt tadpoles hatch about 3 or 4 weeks later and feed on the many small invertebrates in the water.

Hibernation begins in late September when temperatures begin to fall. The newts take refuge under logs and stones, or sometimes deep in loose soil, sitting out the cold weather until the warmer spring days come around again.

Great crested newts can live for over 20 years! They eat earthworms, spiders, slugs and many types of invertebrate, making them excellent garden pest controllers.

These plants are known as marginals, for obvious reasons. Deep water needs a more specialised type of plant, so this is where the native white water lily, with its glorious golden centre went. Plenty of oxygenators were added to keep the water fresh and aerated. Last of all they added a bucketful of water from one of the natural ponds on the farm. This, Heather hoped, would contain a range of bacteria and other watery microorganisms to get the pond off to a healthy start. A friend arrived with frogspawn from a nearby pond, so this was added to the waiting habitat. Everyone stood back, admired their hard work and breathed a sigh of relief.

Within just a few days, wildlife had started to arrive at the pond of its own accord. One of the amazing things about water in the garden is that so many creatures are looking for it, you really don't need to encourage them! The first wildlife visitors were water boatmen that, being winged beetles, can appear as if from nowhere. Later common blue damselflies arrived, stunning insects with shimmering, electric blue bodies, dancing over the water and resting on the new plants. Birds came to drink and bathe and perhaps most exciting of all, house martins arrived to collect mud for their cup-shaped nests which they built beneath the eaves of the house.

Heather recalls how she and Monty watched this process. 'Two of these nests were outside Monty's bedroom window, so we were able to watch the amazing process of nest building just feet from these beautiful birds. It was wonderful to think we had provided not only the nest material but the nest site as well. In the past it was considered good luck to have these birds nesting beneath your house eaves, so, as we watched the young martins fledge and fly away, we took this as a good omen for our new pond.'

Most of the staff agree that the wildlife pond has been the most exciting feature in the entire garden. A pond is a habitat that develops very quickly and over the last three years, this one has become home to a great variety of wildlife and even more creatures have used it in passing. Many species of dragonfly and damselfly have been seen including the handsome broad-bodied chaser. Bats race overhead at dusk, catching the many tiny insects that emerge from the water. Both common and great-crested newts inhabit the pond and Monty and Richard were excited to find their tiny newtlets when they were pond dipping, along with freshwater shrimps and caddis fly larvae. Other wildlife noted includes whirligig beetles spinning on the water surface and great diving beetles with their bubble of air, racing into the depths. The odd toad found lurking in the garden suggests that they too will use the pond for breeding soon. Already, there are more species than can possibly be identified, but that doesn't matter. What is important is that this pond will go on getting better and better, becoming a part of the local landscape that wildlife can rely upon.

LEFT TOP: THE TOADS SEEM LESS SHY THAN THE FROGS
LEFT BOTTOM: RED DAMSELFLIES VISIT REGULARLY
RIGHT TOP: RAIN KEEPS THE POND WELL TOPPED UP
RIGHT BOTTOM: MARTINS BUILD THEIR NEST RIGHT
OUTSIDE MONTY'S BEDROOM WINDOW

Purple Loosestrife

Focal Flower

Tall and stately, a gorgeous pinky-purple colour, long-lived and very insect friendly, purple loosestrife has to be one of the best of all wildflowers for the garden. Add to that the fact that it is also easy to grow and manage, and you have a 'definite must' for every pond.

In the wild this plant prefers to grow in damp soil at the pond edge or on riverbanks, or is sometimes found along a ditch line or simply in boggy soil. It is really very adaptable as long as the soil it grows in does not dry out for too long a time. In the past the flowers were known as 'long purples' because of the shape of the flower spike, although this name was also applied to early purple orchids. The common name of loosestrife meant literally to 'lose strife'. It was thought that this plant calmed angry, quarrelling minds and was sometimes placed on the yoke of oxen when they were ploughing, to enable them to work in harmony.

The seeds of this plant are very small and produced in great quantity, so once you have purple loosestrife in your garden, you will never be without it. Many insects like it, but for butterflies to visit the flowers the weather needs to be calm. A tall slender plant swaying in the wind is difficult for a butterfly to cling to, although honeybees seem to manage very well.

LEFT TOP: WE GET BUCKETLOADS OF FROGSPAWN
LEFT BOTTOM: RICHARD INTRODUCES A VISITOR TO THE
    JOYS OF POND DIPPING, GARDEN OPEN DAY JUNE 2005
CENTRE: CLOUDS OF ASTRANTIA ON THE POND EDGE
RIGHT TOP: DAMSELFLIES 'PARK' THEIR WINGS NEATLY
    ALONG THEIR BODY
RIGHT BOTTOM: ...BUT DRAGONFLIES LEAVE THEIRS
    OUTSTRETCHED, BROAD BODIED CHASER JULY 2005

Every gardener who appreciates wildlife should have water of some sort in his or her garden. Even a plant pot saucer containing fresh drinking water will enhance the garden environment for local birds, and once they are used to this new resource they will visit regularly to drink and bathe. In a pond you find shelter, a breeding place and a source of food for many creatures, so it soon becomes apparent that water is vital to much of the wildlife that visits our gardens. A pond is the heart of any wildlife garden and even the smallest puddle can teem with life.

> *even the smallest puddle can teem with life*

As well as a source of drinking and bathing water for birds, a garden pond will be a focal point for any amphibians you may have around you. Frogs, toads and newts spend a large part of their lives in the water as well as laying their eggs on or amongst pond plants. Some insects also depend on water for breeding, especially dragonflies and damselflies. Mammals such as hedgehogs and foxes need to drink daily and if you are fortunate enough to have grass snakes in your area, they too will use the water to search for tadpoles and small frogs which make up a large part of their diet.

Water provides an important source of food for other creatures too. Many insectivorous birds hunt around the edges of ponds and of course swifts, swallows and martins rely on small winged insects, many of which emerge from water through the summer months.

Why are ponds good for wildlife?

How to make a small pond

There are several ways that you could include water in your own wildlife garden, even if you are very short of space.

• A simple terracotta plant saucer placed in a sunny spot and filled daily with fresh water, will bring a range of smaller birds to drink and bathe.

• A wooden half-barrel or similar waterproof container, sunk into the ground, can be planted with some of the less invasive wetland wildflowers such as lesser spearwort, fringed water lily and brooklime in pots. Add a handful of oxygenators and a sprinkle of duckweed to create some shade on the water surface. Some of the smaller damselfly species could well breed in your minipond. If your plant pots are close to the barrel edge, frogs and common newts will have access to the water and birds will sit on the edge to drink.

• A barrel pond like this can also be placed on a patio. Frogs and newts will be unable to use it as they will not have easy access to the water, but birds will drink from this source of water on a daily basis.

• A small, shallow pond can be made with a piece of butyl or woven polythene liner. Choose a spot that is visible from a window, to give you maximum enjoyment of the wild creatures that use it. Decide upon a simple shape and get to work with a spade, making a minimum depth of about 75 centimetres in the centre. The depth is not exactly crucial, but an area of slightly deeper water could provide refuge for frogs in the winter. Make sure one of the edges is a gentle slope. When you are happy with the shape, remove any obvious stones and cover the soil with a few centimetres of sand to prevent the liner being punctured. Gently ease the liner into the hole and cover it with a layer of soil. Place a plant with floating leaves in the deepest part—a small ornamental water lily for instance. Now fill your small pond with tap water or, preferably, rainwater from a water butt, and allow it to settle for a day or two before putting a few wildflower plants around the margins. These should be removed from their pots and the roots pushed into the soil. If they refuse to stay put, place a stone on the roots until they have taken hold. Make sure you have also included oxygenators to keep the water fresh and provide plenty of hiding places for small aquatic creatures. A simple, small pond such as this will need regular topping up as it has a large surface area to volume ratio and the water will evaporate quickly in hot weather. Use rainwater from a water butt if you can, but tap water added little and often will suffice.

Pond Maintenance

Whatever size your pond, whether mini or massive, it will require maintenance from time to time. Disturbing a pond is never a great idea, so it is best to choose a time of year when you will create the least amount of disturbance for your resident wildlife. October is probably the best month for this task. A little clearing of excess plant growth every year from one area of your pond is far better than a complete overhaul every three or four years. If plants are being removed from one small area, the aquatic creatures will simply move away from your activities and find shelter in another part of the pond. After removal, place all the excess vegetation on the pond side overnight. This will give the dragonfly larvae, pond snails and any other creatures amongst the plant leaves, a chance to return to the water of their own accord. October and November are also good months to remove fallen leaves although you need not be too strict about this. A few will do little harm.

If your pond has silted up and there is very little depth of water remaining (this may happen over a few years) you may need to remove some of the sludge at the bottom. This is a tricky operation and cannot be done without disturbing wildlife. An alternative may be to create another small pond and allow your silted pool to naturally transform into a bog garden. However, if you don't have space for this, removing silt may be your only course of action. Do this gently, taking care not to puncture your liner. First remove some of the water with a bucket or similar container. Do your best to rescue any creatures you may find and set them to one side in another container. Using a soft edged container (a plastic ice cream tub may do) scoop out the sludge by leaning in carefully from the side. Place the sludge onto a large sheet of plastic spread out on the ground within easy reach. Again rescue as much wildlife as you can. Perform this operation as quickly as possible, and leave everything you have removed overnight. The silt can be added to a compost heap or used to start a new pond. This is a process that again can be done a little at a time on an annual basis.

The Hedge

and the Orchard

Trees and shrubs in a garden, especially native species are an absolute magnet for wildlife of all kinds. These are plants that our wildlife depends upon in the wild for both food and shelter and increasingly they are disappearing from our countryside. Hedges in particular are important wildlife habitats—they form corridors along roadsides and between fields, where wildlife can move from one habitat to another in safety, finding a convenient food source at the same time. Once our hedgerows were bursting with flowers and laden with berries but farming practices in some areas have depleted this habitat greatly in recent years.

Trees of all kinds are great for birds; for nesting, food and song posts. A song thrush will nearly always choose the tallest tree around to announce the arrival of spring, sometimes as early as January. From here he can survey his whole territory and tell his rivals that this is his patch. Any tree in a garden will be used by birds in this way, so even the smallest tree is a worthwhile addition to a wildlife friendly garden. The Wiggly Wigglers garden was blessed with a few old pear trees around the perimeter walls, gnarled and thick and full of life, plus a wonderful whitebeam but more trees were needed to provide natural food and shelter. Fruit trees in particular appealed to the team, and a native hedge, preferably a wiggly, not a straight one, was a must.

Planting the hedge

Any gardening activity can involve a race against time and few things are more time dependant than planting trees and shrubs. This is best done in the winter, when the plants are dormant and have a chance to settle into their new homes before bursting into growth in the spring. This is especially true of bare-rooted hedging shrubs.

Without doubt the best way to create a natural looking native hedge is by planting bare rooted whips—small shrubs just two or three years old. These plants are lifted straight from their nursery beds and planted as soon as possible in their permanent places. With Prince Charles' visit to the Wiggly Wigglers garden imminent, this was a job that had to be done quickly before spring, and the Prince, arrived.

At first Heather and the team were rather surprised by the hedge on the plan. We all associate hedges with boundaries around a garden, but this space was already blessed with an old brick wall, which divided it from the countryside round about. A new exterior boundary was not necessary so the native hedge snaked its way diagonally across the garden and provided a wildlife friendly way of separating two areas—the main wildlife garden with its pond and nectar flowers, and the grass beyond where Monty played. There were several objectives in this approach. Firstly Monty's playthings were not always the most attractive items. Secondly, dividing the garden in this way gave it more interest and an unexpected dimension. Walking through the archway in the hedge to discover a different part of the garden would make it feel not just more interesting, but also bigger. Thirdly, it would be possible to really appreciate this habitat and its wildlife from both sides.

The hedge was planted in March, mainly by Jodie, on the very cusp of winter merging into spring. Fortunately all was well weather–wise. A very dry spring would have meant a lot of watering to ensure that the hedge established well, and thankfully this was not necessary. The plants were sourced from a local nursery and arrived bundled together and well wrapped to prevent the roots from drying out. Bare rooted shrubs are best bought from a local nursery as they have the advantage of ready adaptation to the local soil and climatic conditions. The species were chosen to provide colour and wildlife interest all year round and the mixture consisted of beech, dogwood, buckthorn,

hazel, yew, wild privet, blackthorn, elder, field maple and spindle. The team decided to plant a double row of hedging plants as this provides an even denser habitat for wildlife, plus it encourages nesting birds to a greater degree than a single row. The line of the hedge was marked out and holes dug 30 cms apart. A good handful of worm compost was added to the base of each hole and the plants were planted and firmed in well. The soil around each shrub was covered with a moisture mat to prevent drying out and suppress weeds. This would give each shrub the best possible chance to establish and begin its job of attracting wildlife as soon as possible!

Native hedges are very beautiful largely on account of their diverse nature. The mixture of shrubs provides a visual feast, as well as food and shelter for a great many creatures. Autumn colours vary from species to species so that at the end of summer a wild hedgerow is a tapestry of shades and forms. In the spring there is variety in the flowers, leaves and stems, all of which create added interest in the garden. And then there's the wildlife—birds, butterflies, small mammals, bees and other insects plus the small creepy crawly invertebrates that we often overlook, including centipedes, snails, slugs and woodlice. The very bottom of a hedge is a useful wildlife habitat too. Cool, shady and damp, this is a place where things hide and sleep or search for food in safety. This hedge was destined to be one of the high spots of this lovely garden. The alternative—a larch lap fence painted in a garish shade of blue—hardly bares thinking about.

The garden plan included a few more trees. Small fruit trees, plus three silver birches, were planted in the wildflower meadow area. Again these trees were bought from a nearby nursery. Nine fruit trees, which included a damson and a mixture of cooking and eating apples, soon found their places in the wildflower meadow, again planted by Jodie. Young fruit trees arrive grafted onto a rootstock. This is the part of the tree that determines its final size. These were on a dwarfing rootstock, which meant that they would only reach a moderate size as mature trees. Huge, fast growing apple trees would soon shade the wildflowers that were to be planted in the meadow area. The trees were well spaced to ensure that they would only create light shade and plenty of sunlight would reach the flowers beneath. Over time these apples and damsons, together with the wonderful, gnarled old pear trees on the exterior wall, will provide not only food and nest sites for birds and shelter for many insects, but will encourage mammals such as hedgehogs, voles and foxes, which rely on fruit in the autumn as an important source of nourishment. Some butterflies too, especially the red admiral and comma, enjoy the nectar-like juices of rotten fruit, seeking it out, sometimes in huge numbers on warm autumn days.

Since planting, the trees and hedge shrubs have required only a little in the way of maintenance. Since any disturbance at nesting time should be avoided, the hedge has been gently clipped in late autumn to encourage it to thicken at the base, thus improving the shelter it provides for all the garden's wildlife.

LEFT TOP: THE HEDGE HAS NOW THICKENED UP NICELY FEBRUARY 2006
LEFT BOTTOM: …BUT IT STARTED LIFE AS JUST A ROW OF BARE TWIGS!
CENTRE: LOOK CLOSE, THEN CLOSER STILL: BLACKTHORN BLOSSOM APRIL 2005
RIGHT TOP: HAZEL CATKINS ARE A SURE SIGN THAT SPRING IS NEARLY HERE
RIGHT BOTTOM: YOU CAN'T SEE HOW A COMMA GETS IT'S NAME FROM ABOVE

Song Thrush

Everyone loves the song thrush—a bird with an air of intelligence about its bright black eye and jaunty demeanour. This attractive speckle-breasted bird is many people's favourite songster, its rich repetitive voice waking us on early spring mornings. Sadly, that lovely song has been heard less and less in recent years.

A great deal of research in the past few years has focused on the decline of the song thrush. Using records from ringed birds from the mid 1970s, the British Trust for Ornithology found that fewer young birds survived their first winter, which resulted in almost a 60% decline over 30 years. The song thrush found itself on the 'Red List' giving it a status of high conservation concern. Over the last few years numbers of song thrushes in gardens have become stable—gardens seem to be excellent habitats for this bird, having shelter and nesting places amongst dense shrubs, and food for them in the form of snails and earthworms. The presence of broken snail shells around a large stone (a thrushes 'anvil') could indicate that your garden has a regular song thrush visiting.

Thrushes are early nesters, choosing a place protected from predators but with a view of what's going on. The nest is lined with mud, which the female smooths with her breast to make a cosy place for her clutch of three or four blue eggs. She may nest two or three times in a season if the conditions are favourable.

Many birds eat fruit during the autumn and winter months and the song thrush is no exception. Apples are a favourite at this time, when invertebrate food is hard to find. Gardeners can make a huge contribution to the revival of the thrush's fortunes by making sure that food is available over the winter, when the young birds seem to be particularly vulnerable. Leaving windfall fruit or planting a berried native hedge are ideal ways of providing natural food for them and their cousins, the redwing, mistle thrush and fieldfare.

Spindle

Of all the native shrubs that we might see in our countryside, spindle must surely be the most colourful and interesting. It is a large shrub, growing up to two metres or more, and found mainly in the south of the country in hedgerows and woodlands. Where left to its own devices it can form a small shapely tree, which keeps its berries well into late winter. Few native plants can rival it for its amazing colour clash of shocking pink and bright orange. The autumn fruits display these hues, the seeds being orange and the seedpods pink. These berries are slow to ripen which means that they provide natural food when most other seeds and berries have run out. Amongst the birds, robins in particular love them and a single individual will sometimes stake out a shrub, challenging all comers (especially other robins!)

Focal Plant

In spring the spindle has tiny white flowers tinged with green. These attract small pollinating insects. In the autumn the leaves colour up to a deep crimson red, and the orange berries sitting inside their bright pink fleshy pods are visible all winter. The berries are poisonous and in the past have been used for the treatment of head lice.

This shrub gets it name from the fact that the wood—fine grained, straight and white—was used for making spindles for hand spinning wool. All in all this is a beautiful shrub for a mixed native hedge or it could be grown as a small specimen tree in the garden

Birch

Focal Plant

Silver birch is a great tree for wildlife and one of the best trees to include in a wildlife garden. Faster growing than an oak or beech and casting a lighter shade than almost any other tree, the silver birch has beauty, elegance, interesting bark, and it attracts wildlife in droves. This species has over 330 species of insect dependant upon it, including interesting oddities such as the parent bug (a type of shield bug that shelters its young beneath its body) or the birch sawfly larva, which curls its body into bizarre shapes to frighten off its enemies. Many moth species lay their eggs on the birch leaves including beauties such as the large emerald, pebble hook tip and early thorn. Small insectivorous birds including tits, wrens, goldcrests and many species of warbler hunt for insect food amongst the birch's leaves, and other birds, especially siskins and redpolls, tease the seeds from the small birch catkins in winter. A silver birch with a few foxgloves and red campion beneath it make a wonderful habitat for a wide range of insects, birds and small mammals.

BELOW: BIRCH SAWFLY LARVAE ALSO FEED ON HAZEL LEAVES

Blackthorn

Alder Buckthorn

Beech

Plants in the
Wiggly Hedge

ALDER BUCKTHORN   *Frangula alnus*
THERE ARE THREE SHRUBS KNOWN AS BUCKTHORN AND TWO OF THEM
(THIS ONE AND PURGING BUCKTHORN RHAMNUS CATHARTICUS) ARE VERY
IMPORTANT WILDLIFE SHRUBS AS THEY ARE THE LARVAL FOOD PLANTS OF
THE BRIMSTONE BUTTERFLY. SHE WILL LAY HER EGGS ON THESE BUCKTHORNS
AND NO OTHER PLANTS, SO WITHOUT THEM WE HAVE NO BRIMSTONES, ONE
OF OUR MOST BEAUTIFUL BUTTERFLIES. THE FEMALE, AFTER MATING, CAN
DETECT THE SCENT OF THE SHRUB FROM A GREAT DISTANCE AND WILL SEEK IT
OUT. SHE LAYS HER EGGS ON THE NEWLY EMERGING TENDER YOUNG LEAVES,
WHERE HER PALE GREEN CATERPILLARS ARE WELL CAMOUFLAGED AND HARDLY
NOTICEABLE. THIS BUTTERFLY, ONCE ONLY SEEN IN THE SOUTH OF THE UK,
IS SLOWLY SPREADING NORTHWARDS AND CAN NOW BE FOUND IN YORKSHIRE
AND LANCASHIRE. ANOTHER BUTTERFLY, THE GREEN HAIRSTREAK, ALSO LAYS
HER EGGS ON THIS SHRUB. THE TINY FLOWERS OF BUCKTHORN ARE FOLLOWED
BY SMALL BERRIES WHICH SEVERAL BIRDS SPECIES ENJOY.

BEECH   *Fagus sylvatica*
BEECH CAN BE A RATHER BORING HEDGE WHEN USED ON ITS OWN, ALTHOUGH
IT DOES RETAIN ITS LEAVES IN THE WINTER, MAKING IT A GOOD PLACE FOR
SMALL BIRDS TO ROOST IN COLD WEATHER. IN TERMS OF INSECTS IT ATTRACTS
ALMOST 100 DEPENDANT SPECIES. AS A MATURE TREE IT PRODUCES BEECH
NUTS (ALSO KNOWN AS MAST), WHICH ARE A VITAL FOOD SUPPLY FOR TITS
IN THE WINTER. SMALL MAMMALS ALSO EAT THESE HARD FRUITS, WHICH
SOMETIMES ARE PRODUCED IN HUGE NUMBERS. THESE SO-CALLED 'MAST'
YEARS OCCUR ABOUT EVERY SEVEN YEARS. SOME MOTHS LAY THEIR EGGS
ON BEECH LEAVES INCLUDING THE AMAZING LOBSTER MOTH AND THE PRETTY
BARRED HOOK TIP. IN SPRING THE YOUNG LEAVES PLAY HOST TO A STICKY
APHID, WHICH ATTRACT LOTS OF INSECTIVOROUS BIRDS.

Hazel

Dogwood

BLACKTHORN — *Prunus spinosa*

BLACKTHORN, ALSO NAMED SLOE AFTER THE FRUIT IT PRODUCES, IS ONE OF THE MAINSTAYS OF A MIXED NATIVE HEDGE. ITS PRICKLY NATURE MAKES IT AN IDEAL NESTING SITE FOR MANY BIRD SPECIES AND IT SUPPORTS OVER 150 DIFFERENT INSECTS. SOME OF THESE ARE MOTHS SUCH AS THE SCALLOPED HAZEL AND LUNAR THORN, BUT IN SOME AREAS OF THE COUNTRY THE SLOE IS THE LARVAL FOOD PLANT OF A RARE BUTTERFLY, THE BLACK HAIRSTREAK. THIS IS NOT A SPECIES THAT IS LIKELY TO APPEAR ON A GARDEN HEDGE, BUT PLENTY OF OTHER CREATURES APPRECIATE THIS PLANT. THE EARLY WHITE BLOSSOM ATTRACTS BUTTERFLIES COMING OUT OF HIBERNATION AS WELL AS HONEYBEES AND BUMBLEBEES. BLACKBIRDS AND THRUSHES LOVE THE SLOES AFTER THEY HAVE SOFTENED IN THE COLD WINTER WEATHER, AND OTHER SMALL BIRDS, ESPECIALLY WARBLERS, WRENS AND ROBINS, SEARCH OUT THE CATERPILLARS AND OTHER INSECTS WHICH DEPEND UPON IT.

HAZEL — *Corylus avellana*

HAZEL IS ONE OF THE JOYS OF SPRING WITH ITS CATKINS, FULL OF YELLOW POLLEN, SLOWLY EMERGING FROM AS EARLY AS JANUARY IN SOME AREAS. OVER 100 INSECTS ARE DEPENDANT UPON THIS SHRUB INCLUDING THE STUNNING BUFF TIP MOTH. IN THE AUTUMN HAZEL NUTS ARE AN IMPORTANT SOURCE OF FOOD FOR A WIDE VARIETY OF WILDLIFE INCLUDING JAYS, DORMICE, SQUIRRELS AND WOOD MICE.

DOGWOOD — *Cornus sanguinea*

THIS IS A LOVELY FAST GROWING SHRUB WHICH IS PERFECT IN A HEDGE, CAN BE GROWN ON ITS OWN AS A SPECIMEN SHRUB, OR WILL GIVE HEIGHT AT THE BACK OF A BORDER. IT HAS INTEREST ALL YEAR ROUND AND IN WINTER THE STEMS TURN CRIMSON. THE WHITE FLOWERS APPEAR IN SPRINGTIME, BUT SADLY THESE ARE FAR FROM SWEETLY SCENTED! IN FACT THEY SMELL PRETTY AWFUL, BUT EVEN SO THE HOLLY BLUE BUTTERFLY IS ATTRACTED TO THEM. SHE WILL OFTEN USE THE FLOWER BUDS TO LAY HER EGGS ON, IF HOLLY IS NOT AVAILABLE. SMALL BLACK BERRIES, WHICH BLACKBIRDS IN PARTICULAR LOVE, FOLLOW THE FLOWERS. THE LEAVES ARE STRONGLY RIBBED AND TURN A GORGEOUS DARK RED IN THE AUTUMN. THIS SHRUB SPREADS BY SUCKERS.

ELDER — *Sambucus nigra*

EVERYONE KNOWS THE ELDERBERRY, BELOVED OF STARLINGS AND THE CURSE OF THE CAR OWNER! BIRDS DESCEND ON THIS SHRUB IN LATE SUMMER WHEN ITS DARK PURPLE BERRIES ARE SWEET AND JUICY, BUT THE DARK PINK DROPPINGS THEY PRODUCE AFTER FEASTING ON THESE BERRIES CAN STAIN A CAR'S PAINTWORK. ELDER PRODUCES WHITE FLOWERS IN MAY WHICH HOVERFLIES FIND VERY ATTRACTIVE. THE LEAVES FADE TO PINK AND YELLOW IN THE AUTUMN, PROVIDING SUBTLE COLOURS IN AN AUTUMN HEDGE.

Elder

Field Maple

Yew

Privet

FIELD MAPLE   *Acer campestre*

THIS SMALL TREE IS OFTEN GROWN IN A MIXED HEDGE AND COPES WELL WITH
CUTTING AND TRIMMING. IN THE AUTUMN IT IS ONE OF OUR MOST COLOURFUL
NATIVE SHRUBS, THE PRETTILY SHAPED LEAVES TURNING TO A WONDERFUL
BUTTERY YELLOW. FIELD MAPLE SUPPORTS OVER 50 SPECIES OF INSECT AND
PROVIDES NECTAR AND POLLEN FOR BEES FROM ITS CATKINS IN THE SPRING.
THE INTERESTING WINGED SEEDS ARE EATEN BY SMALL MAMMALS.

PRIVET   *Ligustrum vulgare*

PRIVET IS A COMMON HEDGING PLANT, BUT THE WILD SPECIES IS RATHER
DIFFERENT FROM ITS CULTIVATED COUSIN. THE LATTER HAS BEEN BRED TO
PRODUCE A DENSE SHRUB WHEREAS THE WILD SPECIES IS LESS COMPACT.
HOWEVER IT DOES PRODUCE FLOWERS, WHICH ARE UNUSUAL IN THE
CULTIVATED PLANT. THESE ARE STRONGLY SCENTED AND ATTRACT A GOOD
RANGE OF INSECTS INCLUDING BUTTERFLIES, BEES AND HOVERFLIES. IF YOU
GROW PRIVET IN A MIXED HEDGE THERE IS A CHANCE THAT YOU WILL COME
ACROSS THE HUGE CATERPILLAR OF THE PRIVET HAWK-MOTH, A WONDERFUL
GREEN CREATURE WITH PINK AND BLACK STRIPED MARKINGS. THE ADULT MOTH
IS EQUALLY GLAMOROUS! THIS SHRUB ALSO PRODUCES SHINY BLACK BERRIES
WHICH THRUSHES AND BLACKBIRDS LOVE.

YEW   *Taxus baccata*

YEW IS STRICTLY A TREE AND A VERY LONG LIVED ONEAT THAT; THE OLDEST
YEW IN BRITAIN IS ESTIMATED AT 5,000 YEARS OLD. IT DOES HOWEVER
RESPOND WELL TO CLIPPING WHICH MEANS THAT IT MAKES A' WONDERFUL
HEDGE, MANY WOULD SAY THE FINEST. BEING EVERGREEN AND COMPACT IN
ITS GROWTH IT PROVIDES GOOD DENSE NESTING PLACES.

FEMALE YEW TREES ALSO PRODUCE SOFT RED BERRIES WHICH, ALTHOUGH
POISONOUS TO MAMMALS (INCLUDING HUMANS), ARE LOVED BY MANY BIRDS,
ESPECIALLY MEMBERS OF THE THRUSH FAMILY. RESEARCH SHOWS THAT
YEW ONLY SUPPORTS AROUND SIX SPECIES OF INSECT, BUT ONE OF THEM
IS THE STRIKING BLACK ARCHES MOTH, WHOSE CATERPILLARS EAT THE YEW
LEAVES.

Why are orchards good for wildlife?

All over the country orchard trees are being pulled up. Where once orchards of apples, pears and plums covered our countryside, now we are more likely to see fields of winter wheat or rape. Sadly, fruit growing is no longer something that farmers find economical and wildlife has suffered as a result.

Orchards are wonderful places for wildlife of all sorts. In spring the flower blossoms are designed to be pollinated by bees and other insects, so they buzz with life. Many beekeepers in times past would move their hives to areas of fruit trees to facilitate pollination and make sure their bees produced plenty of early honey. Orchards are also good places to find mammals of all sorts, especially when the fruit is ripe. Fallen fruit provides a reliable source of autumn sustenance for hedgehogs, foxes, badgers, deer, and small mammals such as bank voles. Many insects enjoy the sweet flesh and juices of apples, pears and plums, especially the red admiral and comma butterflies and wasps.

> *Just about all our native wildlife benefis from orchard trees…*

And then of course there are the birds that frequent orchard trees, not just for the fruit, (although thrushes, blackbirds and starlings are among the species that rely on this source of autumn food), but also the insectivorous birds such as tits, warblers, robins, wrens and flycatchers. Fruit trees attract an enormous number of small insects, and these in their turn provide food for many smaller bird species that live on a mainly insect diet. Some finches, especially the goldfinch, like to nest in the forks of fruit tree branches and a few bird species, including the lovely brambling, a winter visitor, enjoy the seeds or pips of apples and pears.

Just about all our native wildlife benefits from orchard trees, either directly or indirectly through the food chain. The Wiggly Wigglers orchard trees, with meadow plants beneath, have been planted for the local wildlife as well as the human visitors.

Hedging your bets

If you want to create a natural looking barrier between your garden and the next, you could do no better than plant a native hedge.

Use a mixture of some of the species that the Wiggly Team have included in their garden and you will attract a huge range of wildlife, as well as help to create wildlife friendly corridors between buildings and roads all over our towns and cities. These corridors link together important habitats and give wildlife in built up areas somewhere to live!

Choose your plants at a local nursery if you can and make sure you have a diversity of species.

Once your hedge is established you can plant climbers such as wild honeysuckle or dog rose to scramble through, adding flowers and berries to attract even more insects, birds and mammals. These climbers help to create thick nest sites for song thrushes, dunnocks and chaffinches amongst others.

Larch lap fencing does nothing for wildlife. Plant a hedge, create a real habitat and welcome the wildlife to your garden.

LEFT TOP: BEECH MAST
LEFT MIDDLE: BLACKTHORN SLOES
RIGHT TOP: DOGWOOD TURNS CRIMSON IN THE WINTER
RIGHT MIDDLE: BRIMSTONE BUTTERFLY EGG ON BUCKTHORN
BOTTOM: BRIMSTONE CATERPILLAR ALSO ON BUCKTHORN

Chapter 5

The Meadow

All kinds of wildlife will find their way into a garden meadow—small frogs sheltering from predators, hedgehogs sleeping in a day time nest, voles searching for seeds—a huge cross section of garden visitors will appreciate this environment. As an insect habitat however, meadows really are amazing. They hum with hoverflies, buzz with bees and dance with butterflies. Grasshoppers chirrup, moths lurk and ants scurry about their business. As insects (and other invertebrates) are a major source of food for birds, mammals, reptiles and amphibians, it is obvious that this habitat must be one of the best for wildlife in any garden. Add to this the seeds from grasses or finches' favourites such as knapweed, and it becomes obvious why meadows just burst with life.

Long grass somewhere in a wildlife garden is an absolute must, even if it is just a scruffy bit under a hedge. It provides excellent shelter as well as food for many creatures. Luckily the Wiggly Wigglers garden was big enough to create a large wildflower meadow area. Bridget's plan showed a corner of the plot as meadow with a few fruit trees. It would be contained by the perimeter brick walls on two sides and the wiggly hedge would separate it from the nectar garden. Over time, as the hedge grew, it would be possible to glimpse the meadow through the yew archway. Paths were to be mown through the grass and a sheltered sitting area included in the centre where the butterflies and bees could be observed at close quarters.

Making the meadow

A certain amount of preparation is necessary if a wildflower meadow is to be really successful. Wildflowers growing in grassy places will always look amazing and attract huge quantities of wildlife (just imagine field scabious and knapweed on a grassy roadside) but a truly diverse meadow area with lots of plant species in every square metre is harder to create. Indeed we cannot 'make' a wild-

flower meadow; we can only recreate an approximation of this wonderful habitat. In the wild, meadows have evolved over many hundreds of years with annual intervention by man and beast—hay cropping, grazing and poaching by the animal's hooves. Having said that, a garden meadow is such a wonderful place that Heather and the team were determined to make this area in their garden very special indeed.

Firstly the turf from the designated area was removed and taken away to compost. Turf breaks down over time to produce a good potting compost, and this was put to use later. The underlying damp clay soil was rotovated to aerate it, but it was apparent that it was still in need of a bit of a boost. Worms were the answer and about 1000 lob worms (the large flat ended earthworms that you probably see in your own garden) plus a large quantity of dendra worms (small red worms, brilliant at composting) were added to the area. These did a great job turning over and aerating the soil. High fertility is not necessary for a meadow area, indeed it can be detrimental, but the plants must still be able to anchor their roots in a reasonable substrate of some kind.

The mixed native seed containing about 80% grasses and 20% wildflowers was obtained from a mail order nursery. Extra flower seed was added to initially increase the wildflower content, although over time the 80: 20 ratio usually re-establishes itself. The objective with the extra flowers was to have some colour as soon as possible and create that 'wow' factor in the early years. This would convince everyone that the meadow was going to be beautiful from the very beginning—not just a patch of wild overgrown grass! To make this happen as if by magic, an annual mix of cornfield 'weeds' was also included. These seeds germinate very quickly and flower all through the first summer—red poppies, yellow corn marigold and blue cornflowers—an absolute riot of jewel-bright hues. This was amazingly successful and the poppies and cornflowers in particular did extremely well. Sadly these plants are annuals and are only used in a wildflower meadow to give an instant effect. In the wild they grow on field margins where the soil is bare and ploughed on an annual basis. These are the conditions in which they thrive, not in a closed grassy sward where they are unable to seed and renew themselves every spring. The team loved these colourful annuals and some were disappointed when they disappeared, but over time the meadow established a subtle but more permanent mix of species. The poppies however, found their way in to the gravelled nectar garden where they continue to spring up, refugees from the meadow in its first year.

The seed was sown at a rate of about 3 grams per square metre (anything between 2 and 4 grams will work well). Jodie had the bulk of this job, mixing the seed with silver sand to sow it more evenly. The sand showed up well on the dark soil so she could see where it was going. The seed was then gently trodden into the soil to bed it down. Covering it was not necessary—indeed some species will not germinate without a little light to goad them into action. One further task was undertaken—30 plug plants of snakeshead fritillary, one of Heather's favourite flowers, were added. Choosing meadow

species suitable for your particular soil conditions is really important and these gorgeous spring flowering bulbs with their chequered bells are perfect for the clay soil here.

One of the most successful plants in the meadow's first year was the oxeye daisy. These familiar flowers are often called moon daisies by country folk, because at dusk the flowers glow like the moon. They are early colonisers revelling in fresh soil, and they often dominate a newly sown meadow. Over time they settle down into a more harmonious existence with the other species. This for many people is a real attraction of a wildflower meadow: year on year it is different. Depending upon spring weather conditions, the coldness of the winter or how and when the meadow was cut, the composition of species will vary from one summer to the next. As well as exhibiting a magnetic attraction to wildlife, this is something very positive about a garden meadow; it is a dynamic habitat, constantly changing, a different colour catching the eye every day in the summer months and tawny brown seed heads creating a haze in the autumn.

LEFT TOP: ADD THE WILDFLOWER SEED TO SAND
RIGHT TOP: THEN MIX WELL
LEFT BOTTOM: JODIE, RICKY AND JO SPRINKLE THE MIXTURE ONTO THE NEW MEADOW PATCH
RIGHT BOTTOM: ...AND TREAD GENTLY DOWN

Wildlife in the Wiggly Meadow

The meadow saw a mass of insects and other wildlife within its first year of life and was especially rich in solitary bees. The flowers in amongst the long grass immediately began to attract large numbers of these insects to the pollen and nectar they have on offer. These are the same bees that nest in the artificial bee homes that were put up around the garden, plus those that have found their own homes in small spaces in the surrounding garden walls.

Plenty of other wildlife was seen in the meadow. Jodie made a note of some of the things that she saw: 'I have seen butterflies, moths (don't know the names), dragonflies, mason bees, bumblebees, and a mouse in one of the roosting pockets on the wall around the meadow. In the beehive composter on the way into the meadow I saw a grass snake when I lifted the lid!'

Most of the staff, especially Rachel, Nicky and Heather have been fascinated by the solitary bees that visit the meadow flowers. Wendy also loves the butterflies that are seen in the meadow and Richard has noticed hoverflies, damselflies, various bumblebees, an emperor dragonfly and peacock and small tortoiseshell butterflies. Jo saw a green woodpecker—a very exciting bird that feeds on ants and can sometimes be seen in open grassy places. In all the meadow has been a very successful wildlife habitat as well as a joy to look at through spring, summer and autumn.

Heather summed up her feelings about the meadow, 'For me the meadow really has the 'wow' factor. I'm not into tiny things—I wouldn't notice a single bee or a ladybird, I just love wildlife in bulk and the meadow does that. It attracts so much and it changes from day to day and from week to week. It's fantastic to see the enormous wealth of wildlife there, using it every day.'

Feature Creature

Common Blue

The common blue butterfly gets itself noticed in gardens, in spite of being one of our smaller species of butterfly. Early on sunny mornings the male may bask in the sunlight, his iridescent blue wings catching the eye, or you may notice his bright colour as he flits from one plant to another. Whilst feeding his wings are generally closed, revealing the undersides which are speckled with black and orange. The female is equally beautiful, but her wings are brown with a sheen of blue. Common blues can also be seen roosting at dusk and dawn clinging to long stalks of grass, sometimes in a head down position.

In the countryside this species occurs in many habitats including meadows, grassland and on sunny roadside verges. It is quite a mobile little butterfly and readily colonises new places, as long as its requirements are met. This species can be easily encouraged to gardens especially if its larval food plants on which the adult female butterfly lays her eggs, are available. Common blue favours the bird's foot trefoil for her egg laying, although the caterpillars will also eat the leaves of kidney vetch and restharrow.

These butterflies take nectar from a variety of flowers, but like all butterfly species they have their favourite sources. Wild cornflower, wild marjoram, and bird's foot trefoil are loved by this butterfly and will encourage it to your garden. Long grass in a meadow is useful as it allows the butterflies to bask and roost. The tiny caterpillars also like long grass as they spend the winter deep in the base of this type of vegetation, before finishing their growth in spring, pupating and emerging as fully grown adults in early summer.

Over time

As we have already seen, meadows are very dynamic habitats and can change substantially over time. This is a natural process and the wildlife that comes to a meadow adapts to these changes. There are however certain alterations which are detrimental to a grassy environment such as this. Perhaps the most damaging thing is poor maintenance that can lead to the wildflowers dying out and your 'meadow' becoming a sea of grasses—still attractive but lacking all the benefits that the wildflowers bring including the nectar and pollen that insects are searching for. Regular annual maintenance is the key to a good meadow.

The Wiggly meadow will experience another change over time. As the apple and damson trees and the silver birches that have been planted in this area grow, they will in the longer term create shade that will slowly begin to affect some of the wildflowers requiring a sunnier aspect. In anticipation of this Heather and the team have already created another meadow area using wildflower turf and plug plants. This meadow, next to Monty's area, will remain in direct sunlight and will complement the original meadow as the latter becomes shadier. Many of the wildflowers already there will adapt, but as some species disappear under the fruit trees, the team will plant plugs of flowers more tolerant of shade such as red campion, betony and agrimony.

LEFT TOP: THE MEADOW, JUNE 2004
LEFT BOTTOM: OXEYE DAISIES AND FOXGLOVE IN EVENING SUNSHINE
RIGHT TOP: BRIMSTONE BUTTERFLY ON LESSER KNAPWEED
RIGHT BOTTOM: GREEN SHIELD BUG: GREEN IN SPRING BUT BRONZE IN AUTUMN

Making Hay

Maintaining your meadow then, is crucial to its survival. In the wild a hay meadow is cut, the hay is allowed to dry and then it is baled. Animals, either sheep or cattle, then graze it through the autumn and winter. Most garden meadows can't accommodate this kind of haymaking! We can however, reproduce these actions to the best of our ability.

In October of the meadow's first year a clear dry day was put aside for cutting. This was done with a strimmer. A smaller area of long grass can be cut by hand with a sickle, a scythe or even a pair of shears if it is really tiny. Lawn mowers however are not brilliant for this job as they chop up the grass too much and make it difficult to rake off effectively. Raking well is the key to keeping a meadow diverse and full of flowers. After cutting the hay was left to dry for a few days, then shaken well to get the seeds out before raking it up and composting it. This task is to be an annual part of the garden's maintenance and will help to maintain the diversity of species, and therefore the wildlife that lives and thrives there.

A great habitat for frogs!

Long grass can provide shelter for many creatures. In particular, young frogs often find refuge in meadow areas after leaving the shelter of their breeding pond. 'Frog Day' occurred in the early summer of 2004 when literally hundreds of tiny frogs were hopping around in the long grass! They had all emerged from the water at the same time and had made their way to the relative safety of the dense meadow grass!

Meadow plants come in all shapes and sizes—the only thing that distinguishes them from other wildflowers is their ability to grow well in grass and survive grazing by animals. Bird's foot trefoil is a wonderfully adaptable little plant often found growing on roadsides or in other places where the soil is thin and poor. Equally it is happy in richer soil where it will reach some size, its orange and yellow flowers creating an eye-catching display. In May and June this plant really puts on a wonderful performance, and in meadows and grassland where the soil is really poor, may sometime cover the ground with its blooms. You will also find it on sea cliffs and shingle areas near the sea where it grows with thrift and stonecrop.

In the garden it is one of the most accommodating and useful plants for wildlife. It is the caterpillar food plant of the common blue butterfly and wherever it is grown there is a good chance it will tempt this gorgeous little butterfly to lay its eggs and breed. It is important though to make sure that the area of grass around the trefoil plants is not cut too short over the winter months for this is where the tiny caterpillars of the blue spend the winter, deep in the base of the grasses and other plants, waiting for warmer weather, when it will feed again.

Bird's foot trefoil has almost more common names than any other British wildflower. Over 70 have been recorded and quite a lot are still in general use. Eggs and Bacon and Tom Thumb are the most common, and many of the others evoke visions of past times. References to shoes (Boots and Shoes, Lady's Slipper, Stockings and Shoes) refer to the shape of the pouched flowers, while allusions to claws, nails, and fingers and thumbs (Granny's Toenails, Devils Claws, Crow Claws) draw attention to the five pointed seed pods which turn black as they ripen. Tom Thumb was a small magical sprite and this was his flower. The plant's association with witchcraft or luck is reflected in a Southern Ireland name—No Blame—as carrying this plant with you to school meant that you would not be punished for your wrong doings!

Focal Flower

Bird's Foot Trefoil

Wild Carrot

Wild carrot is a biennial plant, producing feathery leaves in its first year and a branched spike of white flowers in the second year. Once the flowers have been pollinated and the seeds set, the plant dies, but many more tiny seedlings appear around its base. The seed head is a fascinating and beautiful structure, rather like an inwardly curved basket resembling a bird's nest. Once established, as long as there is some bare soil round about it beneath the grass stems, the wild carrot, like many other members of the Umbellifer or carrot family, will continue to seed and grow.

Wild carrot has the flower shape so loved by hoverflies—a flat plate of tiny white blossoms with nectar and pollen easily available. Watch a wild carrot flower when it is in full bloom and you will be amazed at the number of tiny insects jostling for space on the top of the flower. Look closely and you will usually see a single dark maroon flower in the very middle of the white mass. Botanists believe that this single red flower has evolved to attract insects—from a distance it looks as though an insect may be visiting the flowers, which encourages other insects to come and investigate.

This plant had several medicinal uses in the past. It was used to treat coughs, colds and infections as well as being, like other members of the family, an aid to digestion. It was also used as a dye plant.

LEFT: THE MEADOW HAS A LESSER KNAPWEED MOMENT, AUGUST 2005

CENTRE TOP: IT'S EASY TO DISTINGUISH LESSER KNAPWEED…

CENTRE BOTTOM: FROM GREATER KNAPWEED

RIGHT TOP: WHITE YARROW FLOWERS SET OFF A FIELD SCABIOUS

RIGHT BOTTOM: WILD CARROT FLOWERS CAN ATTRACT ALL SORTS OF INSECTS, INCLUDING THIS SOLITARY WASP

FAR RIGHT: THE UPRIGHT 'FLOWER TOWERS' OF SELFHEAL ARE A MAGNET FOR BEES

75

Wildflower meadows in the countryside are fabulous places—extraordinarily beautiful and full of life. They have however, evolved and developed over hundreds of years. We can only hope to reproduce a meadow-like effect in our gardens, but garden meadow areas are still excellent for wildlife and stunning to behold. Even a small space can accommodate a meadow area, but it is vital to prepare well to avoid problems later.

The best way to recreate a hay meadow in your garden is to sow one using a good quality native seed mix, composed of several species of wild grasses and wild-flowers that are suitable for your garden soil. Most meadow seed suppliers will advise on what you need, depending on whether you have dry light soil, or a wet clay. Some wildflowers are very adaptable and will be happy in any soil type. Choose a sunny spot for your meadow and prepare the ground well. It will establish best if the soil is relatively poor in nutrients, so don't use a spot where you have lavished organic fertilisers or compost. If there is nowhere in your garden that fits the bill, you will need to remove the top layer of soil and replace it with a layer of poor quality soil. The soil taken from the bottom of a hole where you are creating a wildlife pond is ideal, so you may want to make both of these great wildlife habitats at the same time.

Ensure that the area is weed free. Take the time to dig out nettles, docks and couch grass—perennial weeds of this sort will certainly spoil your meadow in the long run by invading and crowding out the more delicate flowers and grasses you want. When the soil is weed free and reduced to a fine tilth with a rake, sow your seed mixture at a rate of between 2 and 4 grams per square metre. Sow as evenly as you can, and then firm it into the soil by walking up and down on it and pressing it gently in to the soil surface. Water gently if the weather is dry, and stand well back!

The best time to make a small meadow is the early spring. But don't think that your effort ends there. Your meadow will need to be maintained and this means cutting it at least once a year, sometime after the main wildflowers have dropped their seeds. This may be any time from late July until October. After cutting, with a strimmer, shears or a hand sickle, the hay should be left to dry and then raked up. This raking, which should be done with as much energy as you can muster, is crucial to clear out the debris on the soil surface, allowing the flower seeds to find a space to germinate, and ensuring that your meadow is always bright with wildflowers.

It is important to carry out your haymaking every year without fail then, once your meadow is established, you can add new species as small plug plants in either the spring or the autumn.

Making a meadow may sound far too complicated and off-putting, but take heart. Even if you can't face the idea of loads of preparation and maintenance you can still encourage wildlife with a small grassy habitat. Some wildflowers are really obliging and seem to be able to cope with even the toughest conditions. Plant small plug plants of cowslip, field scabious, wild marjoram and greater knapweed into a sunny area of rough grass and see what happens. In early autumn cut everything to a couple of inches (preferably with a scythe, hook or strimmer) and rake it well and your wildflowers will appear again next year. Don't be tempted to scatter seeds of these flowers onto grass. This never works. Only yellow rattle, a semi-parasitic wildflower will grow in this way and even this is not easy to achieve! Plenty of insects, including some of our most beautiful butterflies, are attracted to scabious and knapweed, and to the grasses themselves, plus the long grass will shelter voles, shrews, toads, hedgehogs and much more besides.

Making a mini-wildflower meadow in your garden

Making a Cornfield

Even a small meadow is a commitment if you want to maintain its flowery nature, but a cornfield area almost takes care of itself. It differs from a meadow in that the plants are all annuals (unlike the perennials of a true meadow) and there is no grass. (Sometimes, as in the Wiggly Wigglers meadow, these flowers are added to a meadow, but only appear in the first year). A cornfield area is simply a sea of blooms—poppies, cornflowers, corn marigold, heartsease—any of the annual cornfield 'weeds' that once graced our arable fields.

> *A cornfield is simply a sea of blooms—poppies, cornflowers, corn marigold, heartsease—any of the annual cornfield 'weeds' that once graced our arable fields.*

Begin your cornfield in the same manner as a meadow, by preparing the soil until weed free and without too many lumps. Sow the seeds in exactly the same manner as the meadow seed, firming them into the soil. Water if the weather has been dry and that's it! The seeds will germinate pretty quickly, except possibly the poppies, as they require a period of cold frosty weather to break their dormancy. Everything will flower for three months or so throughout the summer. In September, pull out the dead flower stalks, making sure to shake the seeds back into the soil. Firm the seeds in again, and be prepared to be amazed again next year. Once in a while you will need to dig out a weed or two that may have seeded itself into your cornfield bed but, other than that, it will continue to brighten your life with its mass of heady colours without too much input from you.

Chapter

6

The Nectar Garden

The nectar area of the new garden was an absolutely crucial part of the overall design. To the vast majority of people a garden means flowers, and a wildlife garden should be no exception. If the Wiggly Wigglers garden was to show people how beautiful a garden for wildlife could be, and inspire them to create their own natural wildlife paradise, then it had to be colourful. But apart from pleasing visitors with its floweriness, the more blooms it had with nectar and pollen, the more bees and butterflies it would attract, not to mention hoverflies, moths, pollen eating beetles and all manner of interesting creepy crawlies.

This area was to be planted entirely with non-native cottage garden flowers, a few shrubs (including Buddleia) and some bulbs. The general idea was to have an updated version of a cottage garden with a jumble of different sweet-smelling plants, all mulched around with stones to give easy access to the plants and a chance to watch wildlife at work at close quarters. Because of the large numbers of wildflowers in the rest of the garden, especially in the adjacent meadow and around the pond, it was not considered necessary to include native plants in this area too. The majority of the non-natives here were chosen for their insect attracting powers, and a few others that were less attractive to wildlife were added for several reasons—their ability to provide colour over a long season (Diascia and Euphorbia for instance), because they had dense foliage for insect shelter (Artemisia and the ornamental grasses), or simply because they were attractive garden plants (Iris and daylilies). In all the glorious mixture of colours and textures, plus flowers over several months, promised to make this one of the most tempting of all the areas in the garden, somewhere to linger and watch the insects and smell the sweet scents on the evening air.

How it was made

The area was cleared in much the same way as the other parts of the new garden. Turf was removed and composted and the soil was dug over. The team had some concerns about maintenance here, after all they were running a very busy and successful business and gardening was something they had little time for, either during working hours or at weekends. To be manageable this part of the garden had to be as low maintenance as possible without losing any of its attractive features. Bridget showed the team a garden where gravel had been used as a mulch and this idea met with general approval. A mulch of pebbles or gravel, composted bark or compost can be very beneficial in a garden for a variety of reasons. In this case a pebble mulch was especially appropriate. As well as locking in moisture, making watering unnecessary and suppressing weeds, gravel or pebbles make an ideal basking place for butterflies. Early in the day these insects need to warm up in the sun's rays. Stones and gravel absorb heat quickly and butterflies can often be seen on summer mornings basking in the rays of the sun on areas such as this. Some fortunate gardeners may find slow worms or, in some parts of the country lizards, using stones and gravel in their garden for this purpose. Gravel or pebbles also show off plants in a wonderful way, enhancing colours and emphasising shapes of leaves and flowers against a light coloured backdrop.

Before planting, a water permeable membrane was laid to cover the soil. In conjunction with the mulch this prevents the soil from drying out and stops weed seeds from germinating. It allows rainwater though but prevents evaporation from the soil. Bridget and a colleague had the task of following their plan and putting the plants in their correct positions by planting into the soil through small holes cut into the membrane. Once all the plants were in place, the pebble mulch was spread. On a wet, rainy day the nectar garden was finished—tiny plants widely spaced with no hint of what they would bring to the garden, either in terms of wildlife or enjoyment.

Maintenance

The nectar garden needs a little maintenance on a fairly regular basis through the spring and summer, but nothing much more than removing plants that have seeded into areas where they are not required. Bright red poppies from the original meadow flowers appear regularly here, their seeds finding spaces to germinate between the stone mulch. As they are attractive wildflowers and have such good quantities of pollen for bees (especially the red mason bees) and hoverflies that abound amongst the nectar plants, most of them are left to their own devices. Over time other plants will need to be periodically reduced in size, moved to new homes or removed all together if they expand too quickly, but by and large, thanks to careful planning, this is a fairly maintenance free zone compared to a traditional cottage garden.

The nectar garden surprised everyone with the speed with which the plants took hold and filled out the spaces creating a sea of blooms for bees and butterflies. It is especially popular with staff and visitors and its combinations of bright colours, hoards of insects and the little added 'extras' (beehive composters and insect homes) give this area a special atmosphere where time seems to pass more slowly and the temptation to linger is strong.

Looking after Buddleia

Buddleia must be one of the top ten plants for any wildlife garden, attracting all the larger species of garden butterflies (small tortoiseshell, red admiral, comma, painted lady, peacock and large and small whites) together with many moths (including hummingbird hawk-moth), bumblebees, honeybees and hoverflies. The choice of Buddleia varieties in garden centres is huge but some attract butterflies more readily than others. If in doubt choose a pale coloured flower—white, pink or pale mauve—rather than darker colours. Although these deeper shades can be grown for their looks they will generally not bring the quantities of butterflies to your garden that some of the pale flowers will.

To keep Buddleia flowering well it should be pruned hard in early spring. Cut all of the former year's growth to about 10cms from the ground at this time. This may seem rather drastic, but Buddleia produces flowers on new wood and the new shoots that appear after pruning will produce bigger flowering spikes. Mulching around your plant with compost, bark or gravel will help to keep moisture in the soil, resulting in more nectar in mid summer.

Hoverfly

Feature Creature

Hoverflies are not only some of the most beneficial and useful insects in our gardens, they are also fascinating creatures too! There are over 270 species of hoverfly in Great Britain and they can be found in any habitat where flowers are present—in fact they were once known as flower-flies. The adult insects feed on nectar and pollen, but their larvae eat a variety of things depending on the species. The really useful ones, from a gardener's point of view, are the species that eat aphids—this is what makes them such useful insects.

Hoverflies gain their common name from the fact that they can hover in flight. They can remain stationary or even fly backwards. Often it is the male that does this—he uses his flying prowess to stake out a territory and attract a mate. Hoverflies come in all shapes and sizes. Many are mimics—insects that have evolved to look like other insects to protect themselves. If you look like a wasp or a bumblebee you stand less chance of being eaten, even though you have no sting yourself. This is why many hoverflies are striped and could be mistaken for tiny wasps, but are actually completely harmless.

The majority of these useful insects are quite small, and are only able to feed at plants where the nectar and pollen is very accessible. Many of the carrot family of plants attract them, as their tiny flowers suit the hoverflies small mouthparts. Parsnip, hogweed, parsley and carrot are all excellent flowers to encourage them to the garden. Many plants of the daisy family also attract them, as do simple open flowers such as poached egg plant, California poppy or baby blue eyes—flowers where the pollen is easy to reach.

Plants come in and out of fashion in gardening, and Verbena bonariensis, sometimes called Brazilian or purple-top verbena, has been very fashionable over the last few years. And no wonder. In the Wiggly garden it has been one of the most fantastic plants, filling the nectar garden with an airy lightness and a haze of purple flowers. Even better than its lovely appearance though, is its ability to attract butterflies and bees in huge numbers. The larger butterflies in particular love it and it rivals Buddleia in its ability to bring red admirals, small tortoiseshells and large whites flocking to the garden. It looks good anywhere in a border or a tub where its clouds of purple flowers continue well into the late summer months, and in this garden it has seeded into the pebble mulch.

This Verbena is not terribly hardy, but worth the effort of a bit of specialist treatment. It is easily grown from seed and once planted out, makes a small bulbous tuber under the ground. If you live in an especially cold area, these tubers can be taken up in the autumn, kept somewhere dark and frost free through the winter and replanted in the spring. The flowers produce masses of seeds and if it likes its spot, it will usually self-seed quite freely. Either way, once you have this special plant, it is likely to stay with you, attracting butterflies and bees for many months.

Focal Flower

Verbena bonariensis

LEFT TOP: SOLITARY BEE ON HOGWEED
LEFT BOTTTOM: ORANGE TIPPED WINGS ARE JUST
ONE OF THIS BUTTERFLY'S MANY COLOURS
RIGHT TOP: RED ADMIRAL COLLECTING NECTAR
FROM BUDDLEIA, JULY 2004
RIGHT BOTTOM: MEADOW BROWN BUTTERFLY ON
INULA IN THE NECTAR GARDEN

Plants that are particularly good for butterflies—having lots of nectar. Some are also attractive to bees…

Allium purple sensation	ORNAMENTAL ONION
Aster x frikartii	MICHAELMAS DAISY
Buddleia 'Black Knight '	
Buddleia globosa	
Buddleia 'Pink Beauty'	
Centaurea dealbata	KNAPWEED
Echinacea purpurea	CONEFLOWER
Erynguim alpinum	SEA HOLLY
Erysimum 'Bowles Mauve'	PERENNIAL WALLFLOWER
Escallonia 'Iveyi'	
Eupatorium rugosum 'Chocolate'	HEMP AGRIMONY
Eupatorium purpureum	HEMP AGRIMONY
Helenium 'Early Sunrise'	SNEEZEWEED
Helenium 'Moerheim Beauty'	SNEEZEWEED
Helianthus decapetalus 'Soleil d'Or'	SUNFLOWER
Inula hookeri	ELECAMPAGNE

Digitalis purpurea	FOXGLOVE
Epimedium 'Sulphureum'	BARRENWORT
Epimedium 'Niveum'	BARRENWORT
Genista lydia	BROOM
Geranium hardy varieties	CRANESBILL
Helleborus orientalis	ORIENTAL HELLEBORE
Heuchera 'Palace Purple'	ALUM ROOT
Lavatera 'Barnsley'	TREE MALLOW
Omphalodes linifolia	
Papaver orientale 'Allegro'	ORIENTAL POPPY
Penstemon 'Flamingo'	
Penstemon 'Garnet'	
Perovskia 'Blue Spire'	
Symphytum asperum	COMFREY
Symphytum 'Goldsmith'	COMFREY
Thalictrum delavayi	MEADOW RUE
Veronica 'Georgia Blue'	
Viola cornuta alba	

The Nectar Garden Plants

Amongst the plants on the original planting plan, these are particularly attractive to insects…

Knautia macedonica	SCABIOUS
Lavandula 'Alba'	LAVENDER
Lavandula stoechas	FRENCH LAVENDER
Lysimachia 'Firecracker'	LOOSESTRIFE
Lythrum 'The Rocket'	PURPLE LOOSESTRIFE
Nepeta x faassenii	CATMINT
Philadelphus 'Virginal'	MOCK ORANGE BLOSSOM
Rudbeckia 'Goldsturm'	CONEFOWER
Tricyrtis formosana	TOAD LILY
Sedum spectabile	ICE PLANT
Sedum spectabile 'Ruby Mantle'	ICE PLANT
Verbena bonariensis	BRAZILIAN VERBENA

Plants for hoverflies—hoverflies need easily accessible pollen and nectar. These plants will provide food for them and some bees too…

Anthemis 'Sauce Hollandaise'	DOG'S FENNEL
Astrantia carniolica rubra	MASTERWORT
Astrantia major	MASTERWORT
Erigeron karvinskianus	FLEABANE
Filipendula rubra	MEADOWSWEET
Foeniculum 'Purpureum'	PURPLE FENNEL
Polemonium 'Lambrook Mauve'	JACOB'S LADDER
Potentilla rupestris	
Ranunculus gramineus	BUTTERCUP
Solidago 'Golden Baby'	GOLDEN ROD

Plants for bees—these plants may have nectar, pollen or both, attracting honeybees, bumblebees and solitary bees, such as the red mason bees. Some will also attract hoverflies…

Acanthus spinosa	BEER'S BREECHES
Achillea Salmon Beauty	YARROW
Brunnera macrophylla	
Campanula lactiflora	BELLFLOWER
Campanula takesimana	BELLFLOWER
Ceanothus 'Skylark'	CALIFORNIAN LILAC
Choisya ternata	MEXICAN ORANGE BLOSSOM
Colchicum autumnale	AUTUMN CROCUS
Cotoneaster franchetii	
Digitalis grandiflora	FOXGLOVE
Digitalis x mertonensis	FOXGLOVE

Plants for shelter—dense foliage, a shrubby structure or tufted grass stalks encourage many invertebrates to shelter including ladybirds and other beneficial insects…

Artemisia stellariana	WORMWOOD
Calamagrostis acutiflora	ORNAMENTAL GRASS
Carex testacea	SEDGE
Luzula sylvatica 'Aurea'	WOOD RUSH
Millium 'Aureum'	ORNAMENTAL GRASS
Miscanthus variety	ORNAMENTAL GRASS
Santolina chamaecyparissus	COTTON LAVENDER
Stipa gigantea	ORNAMENTAL GRASS
Stipa tenuissima	ORNAMENTAL GRASS

Nectar and Pollen

Nature's Harvest

There are many important things you can do for the insects and other invertebrates that visit your garden. You can ensure that they have shelter through the winter (for ladybirds, other beetles and lacewings), breeding places (for solitary bees and bumblebees), water (for dragonflies and damselflies) and food (for all invertebrates). Apart from the leaves of plants, nectar and pollen are the two most vital foods that you can provide, as so many different creatures feed on these important substances. In order to make sure that there is a good supply of nectar and pollen in your wildlife garden you need to grow a wide range of different flower types for your insect visitors, either in a area like the Wiggly Wigglers nectar garden, or by scattering good nectar and pollen plants throughout your existing borders. Even if you only have a patio, these plants can be grown in pots and tubs, providing a mini nectar area for bees and butterflies.

> *Plants with huge*
> *bell shaped flowers*
> *such as campanulas and foxgloves,*
> *just invite bumblebees inside.*

Firstly have a look at the types of flowers you are growing. Do you have lots of wildflowers? These will certainly have nectar and pollen, as well as the kinds of leaves that many caterpillars and the larvae of other insects need. The more native wildflowers you have space for, the more wildlife you will have in your garden. A window box or patio tub can be planted with primroses, wild pansies, lady's bedstraw and many other smaller wildflowers. Next you should look at the plants in your flowery borders if you have them. To provide nectar it is essential to have some single flowered cottage garden varieties. Brightly coloured, double flowers and bedding plants are often unscented and have no nectar. Apart from providing a bit of shelter, these will

be just about useless for insects. Choose your flowers carefully—scented flowers like honeysuckle and night scented stocks are likely to attract insects (moths in this case) to their sweet perfume. Pale coloured flowers, in particular pinks and mauves, are often more attractive to bees and butterflies than very bright colours. And the shape of the flower is important too. Open flowers like hellebores and hardy geraniums have very accessible pollen, so bees and hoverflies will be able to reach it easily. Plants with many tiny, tube shaped flowers, like Buddleia, Echinacea and Vebena bonariensis are designed to collect lots of nectar, so butterflies can dip their tongues in and feed easily. Plants with huge bell shaped flowers, such as campanulas and foxgloves, just invite bumblebees inside.

The more flower shapes and types you have the more likely it is that some of them will have nectar and pollen for insects. And the more insects you have around, the more wildlife of all kinds will be attracted to your garden. Frogs, toads, grass snakes, blackbirds, blue tits, hedgehogs, and shrews—the list of creatures that depend upon insects for their food is almost endless.

Chapter 7

The Vegetable Garden

Anyone who has ever tasted fresh vegetables straight from the soil will know just how wonderful they are—the smell, texture and taste are all quite different from supermarket equivalents, and because they are fresher they are richer in vitamins and other nutrients. Grow vegetables organically and you are in a different league again! But are vegetable growing and wildlife gardening compatible? The vegetable garden in the Wiggly Wigglers garden was incorporated into the overall design to show that most certainly these types of gardening go hand in hand. Making provision for wildlife can be encompassed in every aspect of gardening and the harmony that this produces greatly enhances your enjoyment of the creatures that share your space.

Making the Vegetable Garden

A vegetable patch was included in the wildlife garden for a number of reasons. Firstly it gave the Wiggly team the ideal opportunity to show how growing food was indeed compatible with encouraging wildlife—in fact the kind of gardening they promote works at an optimum level when natural predators are included in the system. Ladybirds, hedgehogs, hoverflies and bees for instance, as well as many bird species, all help to maintain a healthy garden by naturally removing predators, and many insects pollinate fruit and vegetable flowers and are therefore essential to the production of some crops including beans, tomatoes, apples and plums.

Secondly the spirit of community was important. Heather especially wanted to include the team in all aspects of the garden, and reaping rewards in the form of vegetables to take home was a special consideration—another small way of including everyone in the business and encouraging them to appreciate the garden and share in its successes.

Lastly Heather and Phil, as tenants of the house and land, felt that it was important that some of the original purpose of the garden be reinstated. In Victorian times much of the walled area would have been used to grow fruit and vegetables and including some food crops returned a little of the garden to its original purpose.

The vegetable garden area was cultivated carefully—after all, food crops benefit from a good soil and plenty of compost. Railway sleepers were recycled from a previous use on the farm to create raised beds, the soil was well cultivated and quantities of worms were added to perform their magic. Raised beds need a surprising amount of soil to fill them and soil from the pond and topsoil from other areas was used for this purpose, plus large quantities of worm compost and cow manure from the farm. The worm compost came from a former worm cultivation area and needed to be sieved to remove debris before it could be used—a laborious but worthwhile task. The end result was rich, well aerated soil that was likely to grow the best of vegetables with superb flavour.

Initially Jodie, as the professional gardener on the team, was the vegetable queen. Heather and the rest of the staff contributed in many ways, especially with the exciting process of seed selection. Heather in particular felt it was important to have lots of choice—three varieties of French beans rather than one, lots of different types of courgettes, carrots and potatoes, the idea being to wow the visitors, show them what was possible and provide an amazing selection of vegetables. Anything surplus to Heather, Phil and

Monty's requirements was left in the office so that anyone could take home whatever they fancied. Heather found the conversations the next day were always really interesting and loved coming in to work to hear people discussing how they had cooked the courgettes or how wonderful the tomatoes tasted.

As a result of good preparation, hard work and careful planning the raised beds have produced a huge array of crops including four varieties of potato, various types of lettuce, rocket, sprouts, mangetout peas, beetroot, cauliflowers, cabbages, purple sprouting and spring onions, as well as the carrots, courgettes and beans already mentioned. Tomatoes, peppers and chillies were also grown without the aid of a greenhouse. Herbs too were included and the handfuls of coriander, mint, marjoram, tarragon, thyme, sage and basil were all put to good use in everyone's kitchen. There was hardly a moment when something new and tasty wasn't bursting from the soil just waiting to be eaten.

The vegetable garden continues to be managed by Phil the Gardener (Maggie's partner) on a once a week basis. By using organic principles, plenty of worm compost and encouraging beneficial insects, there have been few problems with pests that could not be easily remedied. Blackfly on the broad beans were initially troublesome, but the beans tasted perfectly good, so no one was too concerned. There are future plans to include more hoverfly attracting plants close to the beans to gain the most benefit from these aphid-eating insects. The local song thrush ate the snails and some of the many other bird species around the garden found food in the form of caterpillars.

All in all the raised beds have been a bigger success than anyone could have imagined, and the huge variety of vegetables grown (in comparison with what is available in supermarkets), their flavour and freshness has surprised and delighted the whole team. Even Monty has his own patch now and happily munches on baby carrots straight from the garden.

Every garden needs earthworms—in fact all soil needs earthworms to keep it ærated, nutrient-rich and full of life. They are an extremely important part of the natural ecosystem and vital to the lives of countless other creatures. Many species of bird, mammal and amphibian rely on earthworms as a major part of their diet, from song thrush and blackbird to badger and fox. Worms provide a vital link in the food chain as well as performing an important role in the development of our soil, on which every living thing depends.

Earthworm

There are about 27 species of earthworm in the UK and 15 of these are relatively common and widespread. Each of these species is slightly different in its habits, the way it feeds and what it actually feeds upon, thus occupying a specific place, or niche, in its habitat. In our gardens we are most familiar with the large lobworm, which makes deep vertical burrows through the soil. On mild, damp nights it emerges onto the surface of lawns and beds to search for food, usually leaves and other plant debris. Another species commonly found in gardens, the black–headed worm, feeds on partly decomposed plant material already in the soil, leaving worm 'casts'—heaps of fine soil—around the entrance to its burrow.

Many other types of worm can be found in gardens, especially in compost, leaf litter and any decomposing vegetable matter. Their amazing ability to recycle dead plant material into life-giving compost is what makes them amongst the most important creatures in any environment, and a vital link in the chain of life in your garden.

Charles Darwin, the most famous natural historian of all, studied earthworms for almost 40 years, finding them to be the most fascinating of creatures. In 1881 his book 'The Formation of Vegetable Mould through the Action of Worms with Observations on their Habits' was the first serious scientific study of these creatures. He summed up his thoughts on the importance of earthworms with the following statement. 'It may be doubted whether there are many other animals in the world which have played so important a part in the history of the world than the earthworm'

Focal Flower

Most of us grow mint in the garden, perhaps using it occasionally for mint sauce to complement the Sunday lunch or adding it to a refreshing, cold summer drink. It is however, a much more useful and interesting plant than most people realise, having many medicinal benefits, and it is also a great wildlife attractant, especially for bees and butterflies. Mint was widely used in the past as a digestive—a plant thought to calm an unsettled stomach—hence the popular idea of the after dinner mint. It was also used to treat wasp and bee stings and applied to the bites of mad dogs!

Mint is a native wildflower and there are several different species. Perhaps the best known of these is the water mint, a plant often encountered on riverbanks, pond edges and in other damp boggy places. This plant, unlike the dark green variety in the vegetable garden, has soft, downy pale green leaves and spikes of mauve flowers and it is the powerful scent of the leaves that first attracts our attention. This is a fantastic plant for a wildlife pond, flowering well into the late summer and providing nectar for small tortoiseshell butterflies as well as honeybees, bumblebees and hoverflies. Other wild mints include horse mint, spearmint and a tiny creeping plant called pennyroyal. All have the characteristic aromatic leaves and mauve flowers in whorls around a flowering stem.

Mint

As well as attracting butterflies and bees you may be fortunate to see another beautiful insect if you grow this plant in your garden. The mint leaf beetle is a stunning little bright green insect that lives exclusively on the leaves of mint and related plants. It is shaped rather like a ladybird but its wing cases are a bright, iridescent green—shiny enough to put off predators. Look out for this beetle on all types of mint as well as lemon balm and other plants in the mint family.

Great Tit

Blue Tit

Ladybirds

Hedgehog

Wildlife Helpers

THERE ARE MANY REASONS TO MAKE YOUR GARDEN, EVEN ONE WHERE VEGETABLES ARE GROWN, INTO A GOOD WILDLIFE HABITAT. IT MAY SEEM STRANGE TO ENCOURAGE INSECTS, BIRDS AND OTHER CREATURES WHEN WE KNOW THAT SOME OF THEM WILL WANT TO CHEW THEIR WAY THROUGH OUR PRECIOUS FRUITS, VEGETABLES AND HERBS, BUT IN FACT THERE IS EVERY CHANCE THAT VISITING WILDLIFE WILL BE WORKING FOR YOU RATHER THAN AGAINST YOU. HERE ARE SOME OF THE BEST WILDLIFE HELPERS YOU CAN HAVE IN YOUR VEGETABLE GARDEN OR AROUND YOUR ALLOTMENT…

BLUE TITS & GREAT TITS

THESE TWO SPECIES EAT THOUSANDS OF SMALL CATERPILLARS AND APHIDS, MAKING THEM JUST ABOUT THE MOST EFFECTIVE INSECT REMOVING HELPERS YOU CAN ENCOURAGE. PUT UP A TIT NEST BOX AND FEED THEM WITH SUNFLOWER SEEDS AND PEANUTS. THEY WILL STILL EAT YOUR INSECT PESTS.

HEDGEHOGS

IT'S A BIT OF A MYTH THAT HEDGEHOGS EAT HUGE QUANTITIES OF SLUGS AND SNAILS (THESE CREATURES ONLY MAKE UP AROUND 5% OF A HEDGEHOG'S DIET) BUT THEY DO EAT A WIDE VARIETY OF OTHER CREATURES THAT CAN DAMAGE VEGETABLES, INCLUDING CATERPILLARS, BEETLES AND EARWIGS. YOU CAN PERSUADE A HEDGEHOG TO VISIT YOU REGULARLY BY PUTTING OUT SUITABLE FOOD, MAKING SURE THAT YOU HAVE SHELTER IN THE FORM OF A LOG PILE AND AN AREA OF LONG GRASS, AND ESTABLISHING A SAFE POND WHERE THESE ANIMALS CAN DRINK.

LADYBIRDS

THESE LOVELY BEETLES AND THEIR LARVAE ARE WELL KNOW AS BENEFICIAL PREDATORS, EATING LARGE QUANTITIES OF APHIDS (BOTH GREENFLY AND BLACKFLY). ENCOURAGE THEM BY PROVIDING WINTER SHELTER, ESPECIALLY BY ALLOWING YOUR FLOWER BORDERS TO REMAIN UNCUT FROM AUTUMN TO EARLY SPRING. THE MORE SHELTER YOU HAVE FOR LADYBIRDS IN YOUR GARDEN OVER THE COLDEST PART OF THE YEAR, THE MORE LADYBIRDS WILL HAVE IN THE SPRING TO NATURALLY REMOVE YOUR APHIDS FOR YOU. THESE MEASURES WILL ALSO BENEFIT OTHER APHID DEVOURING INSECTS, INCLUDING THE BEAUTIFUL LACEWING

Growing Vegetables in Small Gardens

Many people feel that their gardens are too small for growing vegetables, but there are ways of including some crops in even the smallest plot. Colourful ornamental lettuces with pretty leaves such as the varieties *Salad Bowl* or *Red Lollo Rossa* can be tucked into spaces between more conventional plants in a border. Carrots too with their feathery tops, look very attractive in amongst cottage garden plants, as do beetroot, chard or radishes. In fact many leafy vegetables add to the ornamental effect in a border and if they are dotted around in spaces, aren't missed too much after harvesting. Climbing French beans or runner beans will grow up a trellis or over an arch—in fact runner beans were originally grown for their beautiful bright scarlet flowers. French beans come in varieties with yellow or even purple pods, so there is plenty of scope for the addition of a few colourful edible plants in a small garden. Potatoes too can be grown in containers and strawberries will do well in a sunny pot as long as you can keep the birds away from them! Use a peat free growing medium in your containers, with added home made compost for a good healthy crop.

> *many leafy vegetables add to the ornamental effect in a border*

Herbs are also suitable for adding to a border or for growing in containers. Chives, marjoram, mint, lemon balm, parsley and thyme will all do well in these conditions and each of them is a brilliant plant for encouraging insects. Chives, marjoram, mint and thyme are all good nectar plants for butterflies while parsley that has been allowed to flower will have masses of hoverflies buzzing around it collecting pollen.

Having a tiny garden doesn't exclude you from growing root vegetables, salad crops, climbing beans and squashes or herbs. If you welcome wildlife and encourage natural predators you will find these plants do well and add to the diversity of your garden habitat.

Composting
...recycling your Waste

The key to gardening in a naturally sustainable way depends on many things. Sourcing your materials responsibly, using peat-free products and demonstrating a commitment to gardening without the use of chemicals are all vital to maintaining a garden that does not damage, but enhances, the environment. Recycling compostable matter is also a key element in organic gardening plus it makes perfect sense to add nutrients back to the soil from your own vegetable waste. Composting returns nutrients and humus to the soil where they can continue to support healthy plants and encourage wildlife.

"Composting returns humus and nutrients to the soil"

Conventional Composting

The basis of a natural, healthy garden is natural, healthy soil and recycling plant material keeps your soil stable, full of accessible nutrients and builds a good medium for your plants to grow in. This is important all around the garden, but is especially relevant if you grow vegetables. There are many different composting methods, the simplest, known as cold composting, being to pile your grass cuttings, plant prunings, kitchen vegetable waste and non-seeding weeds into a corner, and allow them to break down. This has the disadvantage of being a rather slow method of making compost, but the advantage of creating a really good wildlife habitat that is only occasionally disturbed. All kinds of creatures will inhabit a compost heap like this, from the bacteria and worms that help to break down the plant matter to toads, newts, grass snakes and slow worms that might use the heap at different times for shelter or as a source of food.

If this is your preferred method of recycling organic waste, it helps to make sure that you have a good mix of material in your heap. Plenty of dry material such as plant stems and cuttings should be mixed with the more sappy wet material such as grass cuttings. Cardboard can also be included. A good mix is what you want to achieve. It may take up to a year for compost in a heap such as this to break down, but you have the satisfaction in the meantime of providing an excellent wildlife habitat.

A simple compost pile can be improved by putting your waste into a compost container. These come in all shapes and sizes and help to keep the contents warm and damp, thus aiding breakdown. Turning the material from time to time ensures that it is aerated and encourages your plant material to break down more quickly. Bear in mind though that some containers, especially the plastic types, provide little access for wildlife.

Worm-assisted Composting

For your kitchen waste, when you really can't be bothered to walk to the end of your garden the answer may be to use a worm composting kit. These come complete with worms—the main means by which your plant material is broken down. A worm composting system is ideal for a tiny garden as it takes up very little space and can even be kept indoors. This system will keep you supplied with compost for your plants and liquid feed, which is ideal for watering plants in pots or in the greenhouse.

Composting using Bokashi

Wiggly Wigglers is pioneering a method of indoor composting which, rather than using worms and aerobic microorganisms (those that need air to work) to break down kitchen waste, uses a combination of anaerobic microbes including bacteria, yeasts and fungi. This method, which was originally researched and developed in Japan, is now used in many countries to increase soil fertility and reduce the amount of material ending up in landfill sites. The system uses a special bucket with a tight fitting lid that can be used in the kitchen, in an office—in fact anywhere that food waste is produced.

Composting with Bokashi is really simple, the waste is placed in the bucket and sprinkled with a layer of bran containing the microorganisms. It is then squashed down, and the tight fitting lid is added to keep out the air. Two weeks later the contents will not have changed much in appearance, but when placed in an outdoor compost heap or added directly to a border or vegetable bed, the partially fermented waste almost immediately disappears, quickly adding nutrients to the soil. The natural soil organisms as well as your plants benefit enormously from the increased nutrients and humus. As with worm-assisted composting, a liquid feed is also produced and this can be drained out of the bucket using the tap.

Composting with Bokashi could be the perfect composting method for you if you have a small garden, or even no garden at all. Users of the system report that no further compost is needed to grow fantastic vegetables and flowers.

Chapter 8

Adding Something Special

However well you plan the habitats in your wildlife garden and include features such as ponds, meadow grass, hedges, trees and shrubs, there will always be room for something more. Extras such as log piles, bee homes and bird boxes are often referred to as habitat boosters, and they do just that—enhance the natural wildlife areas in your garden by providing a little bit of extra help for your visitors, and possibly encourage your visitors to become residents. One of the great things about a habitat booster is that it is something you can add instantly. You can find space for a bird box or bug home tomorrow and immediately enhance your garden's ability to attract and help your local wildlife by providing an extra breeding place, shelter or food.

Habitat boosters have been constantly added to the Wiggly Wigglers garden since it was created four years ago and it now proudly displays a huge range of bird boxes, bug homes, log piles, stone heaps, bat boxes and of course compost heaps (fantastic habitats in their own right). Another method of enhancing your wildlife garden is to feed the birds—one of the most important ways in which you can ensure birds' survival during the winter or at nesting time.

Where once the windows of Lower Blakemere Farm looked out onto a sea of grass and concrete, it is now possible to watch birds coming and going to the many nest boxes, and some of the bird feeders can even be observed from the comfort of the bath—a wonderful way to relax after a hard days work! Many of the ten or so blue tit and great tit nest boxes around the garden are regularly occupied in the spring and summer. This may well be too many in terms of the territorial rights that these birds demand, but the tiny coal tit is inclined to use unoccupied boxes within the territories of its larger cousins. Tit boxes need to be positioned with easy access to the hole where no overhanging branches or twigs obscure the entrance, whereas the robin and wren boxes added to the garden have been placed deep in vegetation, as these birds prefer a nest box that is hidden from the public gaze. Swallows tend to nest in old barns or stables, where they have access to a ledge in a covered area, so a swallow nest cup now sits in the packing area which is open fronted. Sparrow terraces adorn the house walls and lastly a barn owl box has been placed in the farm barn. The latter as yet has not been used, but this magnificent bird is seen frequently on the farm, so there is hope.

The old farmhouse has a small roost of pipistrelle bats and to encourage them further bat boxes have been placed under the eaves. Bat droppings have appeared beneath one box, which is a sure sign that it has been occupied at least occasionally. The legal protection that these animals are granted means that to disturb them is an offence, so checking for their droppings (which look very like those produced by mice) is the only way of knowing if a box is being used.

Two hedgehog boxes, a dormouse box and various bumblebee boxes have also been positioned around the garden, with varying degrees of success, but without doubt the most successful of the habitat boosters have been the mason bee homes. Just about every one of the staff has been fascinated by the success of these simple structures, which are used so readily by a host

of creatures alongside the red mason bees. Other types of solitary bees, leafcutter bees, spiders, ladybirds, earwigs and a great many other difficult-to-identify insects use these spaces to breed, shelter or to find food in an opportunistic way. Canny spiders will sometimes spin their webs over the entrances to the nest tubes to see what flies their way, and many an earwig has eaten its way into an occupied bee nest to feast on the larvae within. Not necessarily what the newly converted bee farmer wants, but an indication of how the food chain weaves its way through the many habitats in a wildlife garden.

The tubes in the custom made red mason bee homes have a very specific diameter that is designed for this species, but there are now many other types of bug homes available with tubes or stems of varying widths. These encourage a wide range of hole nesting and dwelling creatures and many have been placed around the garden, especially in the nectar area. All bring a range of insect wildlife to pollinate the plants and fascinate visitors.

So much wildlife has found food and shelter in the two small log piles in the garden, that a third large pile is planned for the near future, with buried logs to encourage wood boring beetles and their larvae—a group of insects in sharp decline in the countryside. Also the Wiggly Wigglers garden is surrounded by a high brick wall—a rocky habitat in its own right—where insects such as mason bees may make their homes and beautiful lichens can slowly grow and spread. To augment this habitat, heaps of stones beneath the wooden deck provide refuge for the occasional amphibian or reptile, including hibernating great crested newts, together with small mammals and thousands of invertebrates that only an expert would be able to name.

As well as including all these homes and shelters for wildlife the Wiggly Wigglers staff have an amazing commitment to their local birds. Every week 15 kilos of mixed seeds are fed to the birds around the garden in a variety of feeders at different feeding stations. In addition to mixed seeds, quantities of mealworms, fat balls and peanuts are also used and the ducks on the farm pond also have their share of seed scraps from the seed producing and packing areas.

Solitary bees are fantastic little insects, buzzing around the garden from spring until autumn, pollinating the flowers of fruits and vegetables, ensuring that seeds set for the next year. They do not live in large colonies as honeybees do, but each female has her own small nest where she lays a few eggs and deposits food for her larvae to feed on when they hatch. The red mason bee is one of the best known of the solitary bees and it is now used commercially to pollinate fruit such as apples and plums in large orchards. There are many other solitary bee species too, including the amazing leafcutters. All these harmless bee species can be encouraged to our gardens by providing special nesting sites for them, or simply by making sure that there are plenty of natural nest holes around, in wood, old walls or even in the ground. Each species has its own preferences and a varied garden habitat is

Solitary Bee

likely to provide them with the nest sites and food they require. In addition, leafcutter bees use sections of tough plant leaves (especially roses) to make the dividing walls between the cells in their nest homes, whereas the mason bees use mud gathered from damp places. The greater the diversity within your garden environment, the more likely these bees are to stay around.

All bees, whether honeybees, bumblebees or solitary bees, feed themselves and their larvae on pollen and nectar, so making sure that you have plenty of flowering plants in your garden will provide food for them. These creatures are fascinating to watch so encouraging them with nesting homes and food will not only ensure that your flowers are pollinated but will also provide you with hours of amusement

Habitat Boosters

Bird Boxes

Bird boxes come in all shapes and sizes and the best advice when choosing a nest box is to buy from a reputable supplier. The Wiggly Team have made a commitment to try out all the products they sell and as a result know what works and what doesn't. They only include in their own garden bird boxes that would be really worthwhile and increase nesting opportunities for local birds. Different bird species require different box designs so it is essential to match your box to the birds that you know you have around. Blue tits and great tits are perhaps the easiest species to encourage to nest in your garden, although robins and house sparrows quickly adapt to nesting in a box.

Everyone is familiar with the tit box, which is enclosed except for a small round hole in the front. The size of this hole is absolutely crucial, as is the depth of the box from the hole to the floor where the nest will be made. Coal tits, house and tree sparrows, pied flycatchers, starlings, nuthatches and tree creepers also use a nest box with a round entrance as long as the hole diameter is correct and in the right place (tree creepers like the hole to be on the side of the box). Some other species including robin, little owl and blackbird prefer a box where the entrance is a large square opening in the front. You can also buy nest boxes for owls and other birds of prey.

Nest boxes are generally made of wood or of 'woodcrete', a substance manufactured from concrete and sawdust. Woodcrete makes a fantastic nest box, warm in bad weather, cool in hot conditions and inaccessible to predators such as squirrels and woodpeckers. As well as the standard types of box, woodcrete can be used to make boxes of unusual shapes; for instance wrens will nest in a round woodcrete home with a tiny hole in the front and swallows and martins will use a cup shaped woodcrete nest or platform.

There are lots of species, including the finches and the song thrush, which virtually never use a ready-made nest box, but you can cater for them by providing good, safe nesting places in thick hedges, trees and shrubs.

Bug Shelters & Bee Nesters

Many gardeners like to make provision for the beneficial insects that use their garden, in particular the pollinating solitary bees, ladybirds, lacewings and bumblebees. Solitary bees normally nest in small natural holes in wood or in mortar in old walls, but most will happily make a home in a custom designed bee home. These are available from specialist companies, or you can make your own quite easily. They consist of a series of long tubes of a specific diameter, which are packed into a cylindrical container. If mason bees or leafcutter bees use them for nesting, the ends are sealed either with mud (mason bees) or sections of leaves. However, there are always some that are not occupied by bees, and other invertebrates such as ladybirds will crawl inside the tubes for shelter during the coldest winter months. These homes should be attached to a wall or tree trunk at chest height or above, preferably facing south to catch any warmth from the winter sun. In early spring the bugs will emerge to take up residence in your garden and the solitary bees will chew through their mud or leaf doorway to set about pollinating your fruit and vegetables.

Bat Boxes

All bat species in the UK are protected as these mammals have declined dramatically in the last few years. We can help them in the garden by growing plenty of insect attracting plants especially those that flower, or are scented, at night. Night flowering plants encourage moths which make up a large part of a bat's diet. They eat many other small insects too, so a pond is also a beneficial habitat for bats—they soon get rid of mosquitoes and gnats as they zoom around overhead. You can help them further with a bat box. This may be used for roosting during the daytime in the summer months. As well as wooden boxes, which have a tiny entrance at their base, more modern designs constructed from woodcrete are now available. These need to placed high up in a southeast or southwest facing position, where the bats will appreciate the warm conditions, and they can accommodate as many as forty bats at a time.

> *bats soon get rid of mosquitoes and gnats as they zoom around overhead*

Log Piles

Placing a pile of logs somewhere in your garden is one of the simplest yet most vital measures you can take to provide food and shelter for wildlife.

Dead wood is a really important environment for a huge range of invertebrates, many of which, including the magnificent stag beetle, are suffering from lack of habitat in the wild. Farmland and woodland are much tidier places than they once were and dead trees and branches are routinely 'tidied' away, depriving many creatures of the decaying wood they depend upon. In our gardens we have no need to be tidy in this way, and piles of logs and twigs can be incorporated easily without being obtrusive, unless you want to make a feature of them and add a few primroses and foxgloves for a woodland feel.

Log piles are best sited in cool, damp, shady spots, perhaps under a hedge on the shady side, or tucked back deep beneath an evergreen shrub. At least some of the wood should be buried beneath the soil surface. There are many beetle species that lay their eggs in logs under the soil, and after hatching the larvae chew their way through the decaying wood, breaking it down still further and providing a substrate for yet more creatures to find a home, from wood lice to centipedes. This range of invertebrates provides food for many birds, mammals and other insects.

Hedgehogs and toads may hibernate in larger piles while mice and voles will breed and, if the pile is twiggy as well as woody, blackbirds and chaffinches—birds that sometimes nest quite close to the ground—may find a place to build a nest and raise a family.

Stony Heaps & Rocky Places

While a great many creatures live in the moist shady surroundings created by a pile of decaying wood, there are also plenty that appreciate a warmer, drier environment. Dry, rocky habitats exist all around our homes in the form of bricks and mortar, concrete and tarmac. These in general are rather barren in terms of wildlife unless cracks and holes appear, which may house small creepy crawlies and some plants. Some species of lichens cling to a stony substrate and these fascinating plants provide food and shelter for microscopic wildlife. The larvae of certain moths feed exclusively on some lichen species. Piles of stones or even old bricks in an out of the way place, will create shelter for slow worms, toads, spiders, wood lice and beetles and may even provide the occasional nest site for a wren.

Compost Heaps

As we have seen elsewhere in this book, compost heaps are fantastic habitats for wildlife. They are rich, moist, dark and comfortable places. If you have grass snakes in your garden it is here they will lay their eggs, where the warmth of the heap aids the incubation. Newts, toads, earthworms, millipedes, slow worms, hedgehogs—compost heaps are amazing environments where anything may turn up! For more information on compost heaps, turn to Chapter 7.

Small Garden Habitat Boosters

Even the smallest garden has the potential to house a habitat booster or two. In fact it is possible to include something to encourage wildlife even if you live in a flat. A window feeder for the birds and a tit nest box on the wall outside will bring wildlife close to you in a way that you never imagined possible! Or if you work in an office, see if your employers will allow feeders or nest boxes around the building or bug boxes and bee homes in any outside space.

In a small patio garden, there may be room for a robin box beneath a wall climber of some sort, a hanging bird feeder and a small log pile in a shady spot. Bug boxes and red mason bee nest homes can be positioned on a sunny south facing wall and will enhance the garden environment for you and your visitors. Living with a tiny outside space does not mean that you can't help your local wildlife and thoroughly enjoy it into the bargain.

Make your own Bug Home

A bug home or bee nest home can be easily made and is a great way to introduce children to the delights of watching wildlife. Pack a selection of dried hollow stems of plants (teasels, elder, sweet cicely, lupins etc) plus hollow bamboo canes of varying diameters into a suitable container. This can be an old tin can (make sure there are no sharp edges) or three rectangles of flat wood nailed into a triangular shape. It is important that the container has a back to it—the insects and bugs will need the cylinders of plant stem to be sealed at the back.

Attach your bug home to a south facing wall or a tree trunk in direct sunlight at about chest height. It will be a very short while before mason bees and leafcutter bees start to make a home in the tubes, laying their eggs and taking pollen into the chambers for the larvae to feed upon. In the winter all sorts of invertebrates will find their way into the shelter of the your home-made bug home.

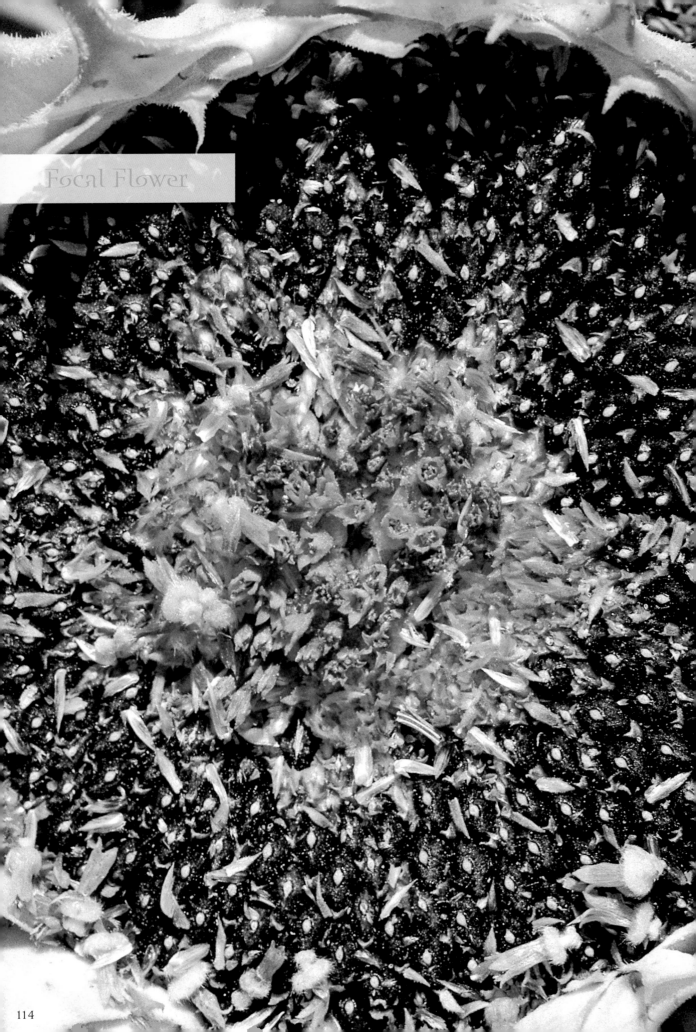

Sunflower

There are a few plants that no wildlife garden should be without, and the sunflower comes into that category. It really is worth its weight in gold, attracting just about everything imaginable from birds (tits, goldfinches and greenfinches), beetles (pollen beetles and ladybirds in particular), butterflies, especially the larger species and bees and hoverflies. It has both nectar and pollen and of course the seeds are so large and nutritious that if they ever get a chance to fall to the ground, they are also a great source of protein for mammals as well as many other bird species including house sparrows, other finches and nuthatches. Hedgehogs love sunflower seeds, as do wood mice and voles.

Sunflowers come in all shapes and sizes, and fortunately most varieties are good for wildlife, which makes choosing easy. Only the very double kinds such as Sungold and Teddy Bear should be avoided, as their stores of nectar and pollen are not very accessible. Although they are easy-to-grow annual plants that can be sown where they are to flower, sunflowers are pretty susceptible to slug and snail damage in the early stages of life. If you have a surfeit of these invertebrates in your garden, protect the young sunflower seedlings with a home made cloche, cut from a plastic bottle, or try a wildlife friendly slug deterrent.

When flowering has come to an end and the bees and butterflies have had their fill of nectar, the seed heads can be left standing until the birds have finished with them, or you can hang them from a bird table or a tree where they will provide your local birds with food long into the autumn.

Feeding the Birds

No one really can calculate the value of feeding wild birds in our current climate of countryside impoverishment. Suffice to say, that the well documented decline of many once common species, including house sparrow, song thrush, lapwing and starling has a great deal to do with insufficient food for chicks at nesting time, plus lack of winter food which can cause the death of vulnerable young birds in their first winter. Of course many other factors are involved in these dramatic declines in numbers, but there is no doubt that insufficient food plays an important part. For this reason alone feeding your garden birds has a huge impact on their survival and well being. It has recently been estimated that almost two thirds of all UK households feed the birds in some way, from those who leave out a few crumbs from the breadboard to others with the commitment of Wiggly Wigglers. Feeding garden birds is something anyone can do, and it immediately makes a difference.

Where once we were told to feed in the winter only, we now know through scientific research and observation, that feeding all year round is greatly beneficial to many species. Always make sure that peanuts are fed in a wire mesh container, to completely ensure that young birds cannot swallow large pieces, otherwise feed what you like when you like. The best approach is to take a leaf out of Wiggly Wigglers' book and use mixed seed, which is customised to appeal to a wide range of species. Sunflower seeds are especially nutritious, being high in fat, and appeal to many different species. Some birds prefer peanuts, robins love mealworms and goldfinches go mad for nyger seed. Apples will appeal to thrushes, and wrens and robins love tiny scraps of cheese.

Clean your feeders and bird tables regularly, move the feeders from time to time to avoid a build up of harmful bacteria in one area and, however you feed your birds, make sure you are consistent. Once you start, continue to fill your feeders and tables—the birds will come to depend upon you. Lastly, make sure that all your birdfood comes from a reputable supplier to ensure that it is guaranteed safe from harmful toxins.

Feed the Birds

Positioning a Bird Box

There are no easy rules about positioning a bird box except to say that if the birds use it, it's in the right place! Avoid hot south facing positions unless they are very well shaded by surrounding trees, and those facing a prevailing wind direction, especially during the spring months, can cause problems in bad weather. By and large birds seeking a nest site instinctively avoid situations that don't appear suitable, but if nest sites are in short supply, boxes facing cold easterly winds or wet southwesterlies may be used with sad consequences.

> " *boxes facing cold easterly winds or wet southwesterlies may be used with sad consequences* "

Boxes for blue tits, great tits or robins are the extra bird homes most commonly positioned in domestic gardens. Tits prefer to have a clear flight path to the hole in the box so when you put up a new box make sure that there are no branches or twigs obscuring it. A tit box should be at head height or above. Robin nest boxes are often well used in gardens. These birds will nest low down, even on the ground, so a robin box can be placed at a height of a metre or less as long as your garden is free from predators such as cats, otherwise head height is preferable. Robins prefer their nests to be well camouflaged amongst thick, leafy vegetation.

For other nest boxes such as those for owls, kestrels or tree creepers check the instructions that come with the box for the optimum position.

Chapter 9

A Wiggly End

Over the last four years and from one season to the next the Wiggly Wigglers garden has gone from strength to strength. It has provided so much to the staff and visitors at Lower Blakemere Farm – ideas and tips that the team have taken home to their own gardens, inspiration for gardens that have wowed visitors at shows (including *Mrs. Warhurst's Garden* which won a Silver Gilt Medal and 'Best in Show' at the 2004 R.H.S. Malvern Spring Flower Show), peace and tranquillity on busy days and a constant source of wildlife interest. In short it has done and continues to do what every wildlife garden, however small, can do: inspire, amaze and educate. As time goes on there will be changes as the garden matures and grows —gardening after all is an ongoing process, and no garden is frozen in time. Every view of the garden that you have seen in this book will be different next week, next year and in ten years time. And alongside the physical changes that will occur as the garden grows, there will be changes in the visiting wildlife as the habitats develop. A garden is a dynamic place. Some plants may disappear and others may flourish, so this garden, just like any other needs to be managed.

There is still a notion that a wildlife garden is a wild place where plants grow unchecked, nettles rampage and long straggly grass abounds between overgrown brambles. While a wild place such as this may attract a certain amount of wildlife, a managed garden with a huge diversity of plants and habitats will encourage so much more. This means that a wildlife garden requires main-tenance in just the same way that any garden does. However in general that maintenance is less than in a conventional garden. A meadow only requires cutting once a year, so there is no constant treadmill of weekly mowing from spring until autumn. Shrubs and hedges are pruned less often to accommodate nesting birds and to allow berries to develop. Herbaceous plants are left standing throughout the winter months—a sea of tawny seedheads for insects to hibernate amongst and where birds can find food. A quick tidy in spring is all that is required in the nectar garden. A little work now and again is all that a wildlife garden requires.

Most of the staff help out in the Wiggly Garden in one way or another, whether it is to fill the bird feeders, or remove the odd dead flower head on a lunchtime ramble. Phil the Gardener now puts in most of the hard work, especially in the vegetable beds which are inevitably more labour intensive. Work in this part of the garden is an ongoing commitment—sowing and transplanting crops, preparing the soil and adding compost, weeding, hoeing and of course harvesting. Elsewhere some of the other habitats need attention. The meadow in particular requires cutting and raking every September and the pond needs any overgrowth of wetland plants both from the margins and the deeper water, to be removed when the wildlife is dormant, generally around October and November. The wildlife hedge, still establishing, is cut back in late winter where necessary to keep it within bounds and encourage thicker growth. Only the nectar garden remains and this is tidied in early spring when the new growth is appearing and the seeds in last year's heads are depleted.

Inevitably the garden is still evolving and in the future there are plans to under plant the hedge with some suitable wildflowers. Foxgloves, greater stitchwort, hedge wound-wort, primroses and red campion would be a good start. Heather would love soft fruit in the raised beds, including blackcurrants, gooseberries, loganberries and blueberries. A greenhouse and some cold frames are also a possibility. A new small meadow using wild-flower turf and plug

plants has already been established in full sun to balance the gradual shading of the big meadow by the fruit trees as they mature. Lastly (for the moment) a log pile of mammoth proportions is planned, to increase the amount of dead wood in the garden—an important habitat for so many creatures.

Wildlife Monitoring

As far as wildlife is concerned, everyone is learning. New birds are constantly seen and identified (a charm of 20 goldfinches was a recent highlight) and throughout the winter the feeders attract a constant flow of tits, finches, robins and sparrows. Cataloguing what is seen is a new initiative to which everyone can hopefully contribute. Keeping records of the wildlife that visits the garden will be valuable for many reasons and information of this sort can, over time, help to monitor changes in the populations of certain species.

Moth trapping nights are planned for the near future and several of the staff want to get to know the butterflies and dragonflies better. Heather is busy learning to identify birds from their songs and several of the team have discovered the joys of wildlife photography. Everyone's life has been touched by the nature around them and everyone wants to know more about it.

Bringing Your Garden to Life

A natural wildlife garden in the middle of the Herefordshire countryside sounds idyllic, and indeed it is. Yet this way of gardening and what it represents is available to everyone no matter where you live. Wildlife gardening is all about making choices—choosing to provide a safe, chemical free habitat for your local wildlife wherever and whatever that may be, where food and shelter are available all year round. And the wildlife in our city and town gardens benefits even more from this approach to gardening than in a plot in the depths of the countryside. Whether you live in the centre of Leeds or the outskirts of Norwich, wildlife habitat is becoming scarce and impoverished. Everything you do to bring your garden to life will be of immense benefit to the mammals, birds, amphibians and invertebrates in your area.

Wildlife gardening is one really important way of appreciating what we still have and ensuring that there will always be some sort of habitat for our native wildlife, as countryside continues to disappear under tarmac and concrete, in spite of the best efforts of many people. So by making your garden into a refuge for wildlife you could be contributing to the survival of some of our most precious species. The team at Wiggly Wigglers, with their dedication, enthusiasm and enlightened thinking have created a very special garden. But not so special that you couldn't do it too.

LEFT: PENSTEMON THRIVES IN THE NECTAR GARDEN
TOP: GREEN VEINED WHITE BUTTERFLY
CENTRE BOTTOM: THE COMMON GREEN LACEWING ISN'T ALWAYS GREEN, BUT IS ALWAYS READY TO DINE ON APHIDS!
RIGHT BOTTOM: FRIEND OR FOE? THE PREDATORY LARVAE OF THE CARDINAL BEETLE TURN INTO THESE GORGEOUS NECTAR FEEDING ADULTS

Feature Creature

The majority of gardeners despise the mole for the disruption it causes to lawns and flower beds, but a closer look at this beautiful little creature might well make them change their minds. Moles perform some very valuable tasks in the soil, aerating it and removing a variety of pest species such as leather jackets, wire worms, slugs and snails. On the less positive side however, they do consume a huge number of earthworms which make up about fifty per cent of their diet and are their staple food source. However, generally a garden can cope with this loss as earthworms quickly reproduce to maintain their numbers.

Moles are unlike any other British mammal and could not be mistaken for anything else. They spend the vast majority of their short lives (they generally reach an age of four or five years) underground in the tunnels they create. Once these have been excavated the mole generally has no need to make more, except perhaps where repairs are needed especially in the springtime. If you do see one above ground however, you will be amazed at the wonderful black velvety fur which can lie in either direction so as not to impede the mole's progress through its tunnels. The front feet are huge and spade shaped—perfect for digging—but a mole's eyes are tiny and its eyesight poor as it spends so much of its life deep in the soil.

Until recently professional mole controllers were allowed to use the poison strychnine to kill these animals, but in truth they cause little damage in the garden. On lawns, simply spread out the molehill soil as it appears, before the grass beneath has died off, or use it as potting compost. If you have many moles in your garden you may be tempted to try to remove them and there are many devices on the market that are designed to kill them or move them to new areas. However, it is worth considering the old country saying that if a mole dies another one comes to its funeral! In other words if a mole is removed another will generally come into the vacated territory. This little creature commands a great deal of respect in the Wiggly garden, having been here from the very start and is still an important and much loved resident.

Mole

LEFT: BUMBLEBEES LOVE MARJORAM FLOWERS
CENTRE TOP: KEEPING A TONGUE THAT LONG UNDER
    CONTROL MUST TAKE SOME DOING! SMALL
    TORTOISESHELL BUTTERFLY ON BEJING BUDDLEIA
RIGHT TOP: HEMP AGRIMONY DISPLAYS ITS 'STRINGY'
    FLOWERS FROM JULY TO SEPTEMBER, AUGUST 2005
RIGHT BOTTOM: A BUMBLEBEE SHOWS OFF ITS POLLEN SAC
    WHILST COLLECTING FROM SELFHEAL
FAR RIGHT: RED DAMSELFLY, HOW LOVELY IS THAT?

Lavender

Focal Flower

There are a few non-native plants that a wild-life garden would be lost without—plants that enhance the wildlife attracting potential of even the tiniest plot. Lavender is one of these plants, as anyone who has ever grown it will know. Perpetually covered with bumblebees, a closer look will reveal many other insects as well. Honeybees collect the copious amounts of nectar that are produced, giving lavender honey a unique flavour all of it own. Several species of butterfly are also attracted to the flowers especially the small, large and green veined whites. Day flying moths including the silver Y can be seen hovering around the sweet smelling flowers. Plus the scent of lavender on the air on a summer evening is something to savour.

Lavender is an easy plant to grow if you have the right conditions. It prefers a well-drained soil reminiscent of its Mediterranean home-land. In a water logged clay soil it is likely to suffer in the winter and if your soil is wet and cold it is best grown in a pot in a sunny spot. Even one plant will bring the insects buzzing to your garden.

And it is not just the insects that benefit from having lavender around. It has many medicinal properties; its oil is frequently used for soothing headaches and tired muscles. It also has soporific qualities, the calming scent encouraging sound sleep. Some migraine sufferers also find its properties beneficial.

There are many varieties of lavender available to the gardener, and all will attract insects. The so-called English lavender (Lavandula angustifolia) is commonly grown but is tall and has a tendency to die back after a time. Shorter varieties such as 'Munstead' are easier to maintain and make a fantastic wildlife-attracting compact hedge.

A Wildlife Garden through the Seasons

What you see in your garden in the way of wildlife naturally varies according to the season. Many birds for example are summer or winter migrants, either coming to our shores to breed while the days are long (swallows and martins, warblers and cuckoos) or to shelter from cold weather further north (fieldfares, redwings and other winter visitors). Many common birds that we see all year round may still have come here from the Continent – even birds such as blackbirds and robins cross land and sea to find a more acceptable environment when the weather is harsh. We, of course are not aware that the robin that sings from our fence in the summer is not necessarily the same bird that takes mealworms from our hands in the winter. The wildlife in our gardens is constantly changing, which means that a good wildlife garden may provide food and shelter for a much larger number of creatures than we could ever realise.

Spring will see the arrival of some species of butterfly, especially those that have hibernated as adult insects through the winter – small tortoiseshell, brimstone and peacock in particular. Hedgehogs will emerge from hibernation, frogs, toads and newts may arrive in your garden especially if you have a pond, and you may start to see ladybirds and other obvious insects. Towards the end of March migrant birds such as warblers and martins begin to arrive, followed by swallows in April and swifts in May. Solitary bees and queen bumblebees will be making their nests and mice, voles and shrews will be scurrying about in the long grass accompanied by the sweet sound of bird song from chaffinch, blackbird and song thrush. Soon the garden is full of baby birds, all needing to be fed.

As we move into summer thousands of unidentified invertebrates will appear in your garden in every habitat. The vast majority will be unknown to you, but rest assured, every single one will have its place in the ecosystem of your garden, as part of the food chain. If you are fortunate, warblers such as chiff chaff and blackcap may use your garden as a source of food, and more summer species of butterfly will appear – the blues and browns, and the painted lady and red admiral butterflies that migrate from the Continent to our shores in the summer. June, July and August are fabulous months in a wildlife garden when every plant buzzes with an insect or two, dragonflies and damselflies hawk over the pond and any outside light will have a wonderful selection of moths around it at dusk. Hot weather may bring a grass snake to your pond and frogs and newts will be leaving the water to spend the rest of the year in damp spots around the garden.

Autumn is a time when garden wildlife can be very weather dependant. If September is warm, butterflies such as red admiral and comma will still be seeking nectar from Michaelmas daisies, ivy and Sedum. Summer migrant birds will be leaving now and as autumn progresses, redwings and fieldfares from Scandinavia will arrive to take berries from a hawthorn hedge or windfall fruit from beneath an apple tree. Many animals including hedgehogs, newts and toads will be seeking safe hibernation places, and queen bumblebees will dig themselves into a small chamber in the soil ready to wait out the winter.

> *And so around again. Every year a wildlife garden will bring more creatures and more pleasure for the viewer. Sharing your plot with wildlife is the only way to garden.*

November through to March is a harsh time for wildlife. Birds will flock to your garden now to take advantage of the food you provide for them. Mammals too, especially foxes may seek food in gardens now. But apart from the clamouring of house sparrows and starlings, much of a wildlife garden will be quiet. Many creatures have a life style that includes a dormant period when cold weather induces a state of torpor, a time when food is unnecessary. Many insects survive by crowding together in nooks and crannies, or have a pupal stage where the change from a caterpillar to a moth is taking place perhaps beneath the soil. This rules out the need to find food at this harsh time. But everything is out there still, in one form or another, simply waiting for the weather to warm up again in March.

And so around again. Every year a wildlife garden will bring more creatures and more pleasure for the viewer. Sharing your plot with wildlife is the only way to garden.

Jenny Steel

Heather's Wiggly Moments

Building the Wiggly Garden took a leap of faith and a lot of time and effort. I'm often asked was it worth it in the end? Well, yes, absolutely. The garden has repaid all our inputs many times over in so many unexpected and delightful ways. Here is a list of some of my favourite 'spine-tingles' from the first years of the garden... I call them my 'Wiggly Moments'.

Wiggly Moment Number 1

"The day that I stood with Monty watching house martins collect mud from the pond to build their nest outside his window, and then we got to watch the young birds learn to fly."

Wiggly Moment Number 2

"Sitting out at dusk and watching the bats swooping low over the pond to catch insects."

Wiggly Moment Number 3

"The day that Monty and Richard found great crested newts in the pond."

Wiggly Moment Number 4

"The day I harvested my own rhubarb for a rhubarb crumble!"

Wiggly Moment Number 5

"Watching the nesting birds and the robin who sits on Noelle's radio waiting for mealworms while she weighs them out in tubs."

Wiggly Moment Number 6

"The day that I harvested my own tomatoes, potatoes and wild herbs with eggs from my own chickens, to use in an omelette."

Wiggly Moment Number 7

"When Jenny came and described the middle of the wild carrot flower and how it looks like a fly to encourage other insects."

Wiggly Moment Number 8

"Studying the ladybirds devouring the aphids on the broad bean plants."

Wiggly Moment Number 9

"Discovering that 75% of our mason bee nesting tubes were filled with a mixture of mason bees and leaf cutter bees."

Wiggly Moment Number 10

"Adding our own worm casts to the veggie patch."

Wiggly Moment Number 11

"Knowing that we need over 15 kilos of bird seed a week to keep our birds happy!"

Wiggly Moment Number 12

"The day that Jenny identified fourteen different butterfly species in the garden."

Wiggly Moment Number 13

"Filming in the garden with Bunny Guinness and for Gardeners World, Springwatch and other TV programmes."

Wiggly Moment Number 14

"The Garden Open Days: we have already managed to share the garden with over 1000 visitors and raise over £3000 for charity."

Wiggly Moment Number 15

"The day the RSPB came and found owl pellets just up in the field."

Wiggly Moment Number 16

"Seeing the practical enthusiasm of all those friends and relatives who helped to transform the old garden into the new: thanks Pip, Pam and Aimee, Ron, Dick and Lee, Jodie and her mum Margaret."

Wiggly Moment Number 17

"The lunches and breakfasts we have had out there, including a drum concert put on by Monty and his friend—the temperature at the time was -2C!"

Wiggly Moment Number 18

"Rosie, Rhian, Pam and Noelle serving up chocolate cake on the terrace"

Wiggly Moment Number 19

"Using the garden for Team meetings."

Wiggly Moment Number 20

"Setting up the stone pile for reptiles and the log pile for bugs."

Wiggly Moment Number 21

"Seeing the effect that the garden has had on its immediate surroundings—birds immediately nested in our new garage."

Betony

Some of the wildflowers in the Wiggly Garden…

Wildflower Gallery

with descriptions by Robert Lee

Agrimony

AGRIMONY — *Agrimonia eupatoria*

ONCE A SOURCE OF NATURAL YELLOW DYES, AGRIMONY IS AN IMPORTANT MEDICINAL HERB USED FOR TREATING LIVER DISORDERS. PERENNIAL, HEIGHT TO 60CM.

BETONY — *Stachys officinalis*

BETONY GROWS NATURALLY IN OPEN WOODLAND, IN HEDGEROWS AND ON GRASSLANDS. IT WAS USED BY THE MEDIÆVAL HERBALISTS AS ONE OF THE GREAT 'ALL-HEALS'. WILL ESTABLISH IN EITHER SUN OR SHADE AND PRODUCES PURPLE FLOWERS FROM JUNE TO SEPTEMBER. PERENNIAL, HEIGHT TO 50CM.

BILBERRY (WHINBERRY) — *Vaccinium myrtillus*

PERENNIAL, GROWING TO 30CM IN HEIGHT AND OCCASIONALLY MORE. ANOTHER PLANT THAT DEFINITELY REQUIRES ACID SOILS. THE BLUE-BLACK BERRIES HAVE A BLOOM LIKE A PLUM AND A DELICIOUS FLAVOUR USED IN CRUMBLES, PIES, MUFFINS AND WINE MAKING. A NICE ADDITION TO THE HEATHER GARDEN OR PLANT IN TUBS.

BUR REED — *Sparganium erectum*

THIS PERENNIAL PLANT GROWS IN THE SHALLOW WATER OF PONDS, DITCHES, AND SLOW MOVING RIVERS. IT REACHES UP TO 1 METRE IN HEIGHT. THE FLOWERING SPIKE HAS MALE FLOWERS AT THE TOP AND YELLOW/BROWN FEMALE FLOWERS AT THE BOTTOM, WHICH PRODUCE ROUND GREEN SEED HEADS LIKE A SPIKY GOLF BALL.

CORN MINT — *Mentha arvensis*

PERENNIAL, 10 TO 45CM. GROWS IN FIELDS AND OPEN WOODS. VERY AROMATIC LEAVES. BLUEISH PURPLE FLOWERS FROM JULY TO OCTOBER ARE PRODUCED IN WHORLS AROUND THE LEAF AXILS AND NOT AT THE END OF THE STEMS LIKE MOST OTHER MINTS.

COTTONGRASS — *Eriophorum angustifolium*

PERENNIAL, 20 TO 60CM IN HEIGHT. COTTONGRASS GROWS BEST IN WET, ACID SOILS, EVEN BOGS. IT GETS ITS COMMON NAME FROM THE COTTON LIKE SEEDHEADS. BESIDES BEING A RATHER SPECTACULAR LOOKING FLOWER, COTTONGRASS IS THE PLANT ON WHICH THE LARGE HEATH BUTTERFLY LAYS ITS EGGS. ALTHOUGH THE LARGE HEATH IS WIDESPREAD OVER MUCH OF IRELAND, SCOTLAND AND NORTHERN ENGLAND IT'S NOT SO WELL KNOWN AS IT PREFERS TO LIVE ON WILD, BOGGY MOORLAND BUT THEN, WHO KNOWS, PERHAPS THAT'S THE DESCRIPTION OF YOUR GARDEN!

Corn Mint

Bilberry

Bur Reed

Cottongrass

Cowberry

Devilsbit Scabious

Cowslip

COWBERRY (RED) — *Vaccinium vitis-idaea*
PERENNIAL TO 30CM IN HEIGHT AND FLOWERS IN APRIL TO JUNE. THE RED BERRIES, WHICH APPEAR IN AUGUST HAVE A VERY HIGH VITAMIN C CONTENT. GROWS IN ACID SOIL.

COWSLIP — *Primula veris*
ITS BEAUTIFUL YELLOW SPRING FLOWERS MAKE THIS AN EASY CHOICE FOR ANY GARDEN BUT COWSLIP ALSO IS A VITAL FOOD PLANT FOR SEVERAL BUTTERFLIES AND MOTHS. THE RARE 'DUKE OF BURGUNDY' BUTTERFLY LAYS ITS EGGS ON EITHER PRIMROSE OR COWSLIP. PERENNIAL, HEIGHT TO 30CM.

DEVILSBIT SCABIOUS — *Succisa pratensis*
ITS NAME COMES FROM FOLKLORE THAT CLAIMED THE DEVIL HAD BITTEN OFF ITS ROOTS. QUITE HAPPY IN DAMP AREAS. AS A RICH NECTAR SOURCE IT'S A GOOD BEE AND BUTTERFLY PLANT AND, LATER IN THE YEAR, ITS SEED IS POPULAR WITH FINCHES. ITS LEAVES ARE THE CHOSEN SPOT FOR MARSH FRITILLARY BUTTERFLIES TO LAY THEIR EGGS, BUT YOU'LL HAVE TO LOOK CLOSELY TO SEE THEM AS THEY ARE LESS THAN 1MM ACROSS AND THE BUTTERFLY IS RATHER RARE. PERENNIAL, HEIGHT TO 80CM.

DOG VIOLET — *Viola canina*
THE COMMONEST BRITISH VIOLET. A PERENNIAL PLANT OF WOODLAND AND HEDGEROWS, GROWING TO 20CM IN HEIGHT. PRODUCES MASSES OF BLUE TO WHITE FLOWERS IN EARLY SPRING AND IS A FOOD PLANT FOR FRITILLARY BUTTERFLIES. IT WAS GIVEN THE NAME DOG VIOLET BECAUSE, BEING SCENTLESS, IT WAS CONSIDERED FIT ONLY FOR DOGS!

FIELD SCABIOUS — *Knautia arvensis*
UNLIKE THE DAMP LOVING DEVIL'S BIT SCABIOUS, THIS IS THE ONE TO PLANT IN THE DRIER PARTS OF YOUR GARDEN. BUTTERFLIES AND BEES WILL QUEUE TO DRINK FROM ITS RICH NECTAR SOURCE. ITS SOFT LILAC-BLUE FLOWERS FEATURE DISTINCTIVE LONG STAMENS THAT SHED RED POLLEN DUST IN SUMMER AND AUTUMN. PERENNIAL, HEIGHT TO 80CM.

FLEABANE — *Pulicaria dysentarica*
IN FLOWER FROM AUGUST TO SEPTEMBER WITH THE SEEDS RIPENING INTO OCTOBER. FLEABANE, A YELLOW DAISY, LOOKS A LOT LIKE AN OLD-FASHIONED MARIGOLD. IT IS POLLINATED BY FLIES AS WELL AS BEES AND IS NOT FOUND IN THE NORTH OF SCOTLAND. PREFERS GENERALLY WET AREAS, AVOIDING CALCAREOUS SOILS BUT VERY HAPPY ON CLAY. PERENNIAL, TO 40CM.

FLOWERING RUSH — *Butomus umbellatus*
A STRIKING, ERECT PERENNIAL. ITS HANDSOME APPEARANCE MAKES IT A POPULAR 'RUSH' FOR GARDEN PLANTING. PRODUCES DOMES OF PINK FLOWERS FROM JULY TO SEPTEMBER. GROWS TO 1.5M TALL.

Dog Violet

Fleabane

Field Scabious

Flowering Rush

Foxglove

Greater Spearwort

Greater Knapweed

FOXGLOVE   *Digitalis purpurea*
THE TALL AND ELEGANT PINK FLOWERED FOXGLOVE IS THE SOURCE OF
THE POWERFUL HEART DRUG DIGITALIS, BUT IS OTHERWISE POISONOUS.
POLLINATED BY BUMBLEBEES. BIENNIAL, HEIGHT TO 1.5M.

GREATER KNAPWEED   *Centaurea scabiosa*
A SUPER PLANT FOR BUTTERFLIES, FLOWERING THROUGHOUT THE SUMMER
AND AUTUMN THEN PRODUCING PLENTY OF SEEDS FOR SEED EATING BIRDS.
PERENNIAL, HEIGHT TO 80CM.

GREATER SPEARWORT   *Ranunculus lingua*
SIMILAR TO THE LESSER SPEARWORT BUT LARGER IN EVERY WAY... LONGER
STEMS AND LEAVES WITH LARGER NECTAR RICH FLOWERS. HAPPIEST GROWING
IN DEEPER WATER UP TO 30CM DEEP. PERENNIAL.

GIPSYWORT   *Lycopus europaeus*
HARDY PERENNIAL GROWING TO 1M. IN FLOWER FROM JUNE TO SEPTEMBER.
THE SMALL, WHITE FLOWERS ARE HERMAPHRODITE AND ARE POLLINATED BY
BEES AND FLIES. GROWS VIGOROUSLY TO 40CM BY 90CM AND MAY NEED TO
BE CONTROLLED.

HAREBELL   *Campanula rotundifolia*
THE SCOTTISH BLUEBELL GROWS BEST ON DRY SOILS, ESPECIALLY IN THE
NORTH. PRODUCES HOSTS OF GLORIOUS BLUE BELL-SHAPED FLOWERS WHEN
PLANTED IN DRIFTS. ALTHOUGH THE STEM LEAVES ARE LONG AND THIN THE
NAME 'ROTUNDIFOLIA' REFERS TO THE SMALL, ROUND, LOWER LEAVES.
PERENNIAL TO 25CM.

HEATHER   *Calluna vulgaris*
PERENNIAL, GROWING 20 TO 40CM IN HEIGHT. HEATHER FAMOUSLY PREFERS
ACID SOILS IN HEATHS, MOORS, BOGS AND WOODLAND AND REQUIRES
SIMILARLY ACID SOIL IN YOUR GARDEN, SO CHECK YOUR SOIL'S PH BEFORE
ORDERING (OR PLANT IN A POT OF ERICACEOUS COMPOST). PRODUCES MASSES
OF PURPLE FLOWERS DURING THE HIGH SUMMER WHICH ARE POLLINATED BY
BEES TO PRODUCE THE FAMOUS HEATHER HONEY.

HEMP AGRIMONY   *Eupatorium cannabinum*
HARDY PERENNIAL GROWING TO 1.2M. IN FLOWER FROM JULY TO SEPTEMBER.
THE SCENTED FLOWERS ARE FULL OF NECTAR AND ATTRACT BEES, FLIES,
BEETLES, MOTHS AND BUTTERFLIES. AVOID PLANTING HEMP AGRIMONY ON
ACID SOILS.

Gipsywort

Heather

Harebell

Hemp Agrimony

Lady's Bedstraw

Lesser Knapweed

Lady's Smock

LADY'S BEDSTRAW
Galium verum

A PERENNIAL PLANT OF MEADOWS AND HEDGEROWS, WITH TRAILING STEMS GROWING THROUGH THE GRASS THAT SUPPORT THE YELLOW FLOWERS. THE PLANT'S SWEET HAY SCENT MADE IT A POPULAR FOR FILLING MATTRESSES.

LADY'S SMOCK
Cardamine pratensis

LADY'S SMOCK IS ALSO KNOWN AS THE 'CUCKOO FLOWER' AS IT FLOWERS FROM THE ARRIVAL TO THE DEPARTURE OF ADULT CUCKOOS, IE. APRIL TO JULY. THE LOWER LEAVES CAN BE EATEN AND TASTE A LITTLE LIKE WATERCRESS. WHETHER ORANGE-TIP BUTTERFLIES LIKE THE TASTE OF WATERCRESS IS UNKNOWN, BUT THEY DO SEEM TO LIKE THE TASTE OF LADY'S SMOCK AS THIS IS WHERE, FROM MAY ONWARDS, THEY LAY THEIR EGGS. PERENNIAL, FLOWERING STEMS 30 TO 45 CM.

LESSER KNAPWEED
Centaurea nigra

A COMMON BRITISH NATIVE, EXCEPT IN THE HIGHLANDS. ANOTHER MEDICINAL PLANT, THIS ONE WAS USED TO TREAT BRUISES AND WOUNDS WHILST THE FLOWER TOPS HAVE BEEN USED TO MAKE A YELLOW/GREEN DYE. THE DRIED FLOWER HEADS ARE POPULAR WITH FLOWER ARRANGERS. PERENNIAL, TO 50 CM.

LESSER REEDMACE
Typha angustifolia

SMALLER THAN THE BULRUSH OR REEDMACE WITH MALE AND FEMALE FLOWERS SEPARATED FROM EACH OTHER ON THE FLOWER STEM BY ABOUT 5 CM, THIS CAN STILL GROW INTO A FAIR SIZED PLANT. PERENNIAL TO 2 M TALL.

LESSER SPEARWORT
Ranunculus flammula

LONG, TRAILING STEMS (TO 60 CM) AND FLOWERING RIGHT THROUGH FROM MAY TO SEPTEMBER THE SPEARWORT WAS ONCE USED AS A BIZARRE 'REMEDY' FOR PLAGUE SORES. POISONOUS. PERENNIAL.

MAIDEN PINK
Dianthus deltoides

PERENNIAL, WITH STEMS 20-45 CM HIGH. A PLANT OF DRY GRASSLAND WHICH PRODUCES BEAUTIFUL PINK FLOWERS, SAID TO BE THE SAME AS A BLUSHING MAIDEN, ALTHOUGH THE FLOWERS MAY OCCASIONALLY BE WHITE. A FLOWERING TIME FROM JUNE TO SEPTEMBER IS ONE OF THE LONGEST OF ALL OUR NATIVE PLANTS.

MARSH BEDSTRAW
Galium palustre

PERENNIAL. CREEPING STEMS UP TO 1 M FIND SUPPORT FROM SURROUNDING PLANTS. CAN LOOK VERY EFFECTIVE WITH A SPLASH OF WHITE FLOWERS FROM MAY TO JUNE MIXING WITH THE VEGETATION IT GROWS THROUGH.

Lesser Reedmace

Maiden
Pink

Lesser
Spearwort

Marsh
Bedstraw

Marsh Cinquefoil

Marsh Woundwort

Marsh Marigold

MARSH CINQUEFOIL — *Potentilla palustris*

PERENNIAL. STEMS UP TO 45CM WITH A VERY STRIKING PURPLE FLOWER, WHICH TURNS INTO A FRUITING BODY THAT LOOKS RATHER LIKE A STRAWBERRY. AN IDEAL PLANT FOR THE BOG GARDEN OR LARGE POND.

MARSH MARIGOLD — *Caltha palustris*

A NECTAR RICH PERENNIAL. IN FLOWER FROM MARCH TO JULY SO PROVIDING EARLY NECTAR AND POLLEN. THE FLOWERS ARE POLLINATED BY BEES, BEETLES AND FLIES. MARSH MARIGOLD SEEDS FLOAT SO THEY EVENTUALLY FIND THEIR WAY TO THE BANKS OF THE WATER SOURCE. GROWS TO 40CM.

MARSH WOUNDWORT — *Stachys palustris*

MARSH WOUNDWORT GROWS, AS ITS MARSHY NAME SUGGESTS, BY PONDS, STREAMS, RIVERS, MARSHES AND FENS. IT CAN GROW QUITE TALL, REACHING A HEIGHT OF UP TO 80CM, BUT IS OFTEN MUCH LESS. IT PRODUCES MASSES OF ITS PINKY-RED FLOWERS FROM JUNE TO LATE AUTUMN PROVIDING AN IMPORTANT LATE NECTAR SOURCE FOR BEES. AN EYE-CATCHER WELL WORTHY OF A PLACE BY YOUR POND. PERENNIAL.

MEADOW SAXIFRAGE — *Saxifraga granulata*

A PLANT OF HILLS AND MEADOWS PRODUCING WHITE FLOWERS ON STEMS 30-40CM IN HEIGHT IN APRIL TO JUNE. AN UNCOMMON PLANT DESPITE PRODUCING MASSES OF TINY SEEDS AND FORMING BULBILS AT THE BASE OF ITS STEM. PERENNIAL.

MEADOWSWEET — *Filipendula ulmaria*

IN FLOWER FROM JUNE TO AUGUST. THE SCENTED FLOWERS ARE POLLINATED BY BEES, FLIES AND BEETLES. NOT SUITABLE FOR ACID SOILS. YOU'LL LOVE THE CONSTANT HUM OF HOVERFLIES AND BEES SWARMING ON THE SWEETLY SCENTED FLOWERS. IT'S ALSO ONE OF THE LARVAL FOOD PLANTS FOR THE EMPEROR MOTH. GROWS TO 1.2M.

MUSK MALLOW — *Malva moschata*

A GARDEN FAVOURITE FOR ITS PASTEL PINK FLOWERS THAT APPEAR IN THE SUMMER AND AUTUMN. A GOOD NECTAR PLANT FOR BEES. PERENNIAL, HEIGHT TO 70CM.

OXEYE DAISY — *Leucanthemum vulgare*

OXEYE DAISIES ARE POPULAR WITH MASON BEES AND HOVERFLIES. A PROLIFIC SEED PRODUCER SO IT CAN SPREAD TO COLONISE ALL THE SUNNY AREAS OF YOUR GARDEN. PERENNIAL, HEIGHT TO 60CM.

Meadow Saxifrage

Musk Mallow

Meadowsweet

Oxeye Daisy

Primrose

Red Campion

Ragged Robin

PRIMROSE *Primula vulgaris*
NAMED THE 'FIRST ROSE' THE PRIMA ROSA GROWS WILD IN EARLY SPRING IN WOODLAND AND UNDER SHADY HEDGES. PERENNIAL, HEIGHT TO 20CM.

RAGGED ROBIN *Lychnis flos-cuculi*
THIS LATE SPRING FLOWERING FAVOURITE TAKES ITS NAME FROM ITS MUCH-DIVIDED, THREAD-LIKE PETALS. GROWS BEST IN REALLY DAMP MEADOWS, MARSHES AND FENS. CAMPION AND LYCHNIS MOTHS IN PARTICULAR LOVE IT. PERENNIAL, HEIGHT TO 50CM.

RED CAMPION *Silene dioica*
RED CAN HYBRIDISE WITH WHITE CAMPION TO GIVE PINK FLOWERS. CAN FLOWER FROM EARLY SUMMER THROUGH TO LATE AUTUMN. GROWS BEST IN SHADY PLACES. PERENNIAL, HEIGHT TO 80CM.

ROCK ROSE *Helianthemum nummularium*
ROCK ROSE STEMS ARE UP TO 30CM LONG AND CREEP ALONG THE GROUND. IT FLOWERS FROM MAY TO AUGUST, BUT THESE OPEN ONLY IN FULL SUN. THIS BEAUTIFUL WILDFLOWER IS ACTUALLY A DECIDUOUS SHRUB AND IS BEST GROWN IN A ROCKERY OR DRY BANK, WHERE IT WILL ATTRACT BLUE BUTTERFLIES. FROM THE MIDLANDS SOUTH IT IS ALSO A FAVOURED FOOD PLANT FOR THE BROWN ARGUS (WHICH IS, CONFUSINGLY ENOUGH, A 'BLUE' BUTTERFLY, ALTHOUGH IT IS BROWN IN COLOUR). PERENNIAL.

SALAD BURNET *Sanguisorba minor*
PERENNIAL. THRIVES IN ANY NEUTRAL SOIL WHERE IT GROWS TO 25CM IN HEIGHT BEFORE PRODUCING ITS CURIOUS FLOWER HEADS. THESE APPEAR FROM MAY TO AUGUST AND HAVE FEMALE PARTS AT THE TOP AND MALE AT THE BOTTOM. THERE ARE NO PETALS, JUST A GREEN CALYX WITH RED FEMALE STIGMAS AND LONG STALKED MALE STAMENS. THESE DON'T PRODUCE ANY NECTAR AS POLLINATION IS BY WIND. SALAD BURNET LEAVES CAN BE ADDED (SPARINGLY) TO SALADS TO GIVE THEM A KICK OR TO HELP FLAVOUR WINE.

SELFHEAL *Prunella vulgaris*
A VERY COMMON PERENNIAL AND ANOTHER EXCELLENT NECTAR PLANT ALTHOUGH IT TENDS TO BE MOST ATTRACTIVE TO THE SMALLER SPECIES OF BEE. THE NAME REFLECTS A LONG HISTORY OF USE BY HERBALISTS FOR STAUNCHING WOUNDS. LOVELY, RICH PURPLE FLOWERS. HEIGHT TO 20CM ALTHOUGH OFTEN LESS.

SHEEPSBIT SCABIOUS *Jasione montana*
SHEEPSBIT MAY LOOK LIKE A SCABIOUS BUT BOTANISTS HAVE DISCOVERED THAT IT IS IN FACT FROM A DIFFERENT FAMILY OF PLANTS ALTOGETHER. IT FLOWERS FROM JUNE TO SEPTEMBER, USUALLY ON LIME FREE SOILS. ANNUAL OR SHORT LIVED PERENNIAL, HEIGHT TO 50CM. RICH NECTAR SOURCE.

Rock Rose

Selfheal

Salad
Burnet

Sheepsbit
Scabious

143

Snake's Head Fritillary

Skullcap

Small Scabious

SKULLCAP — *Scutellaria galericulata*

PERENNIAL. PRODUCES BLUE FLOWERS IN THE LEAF AXILS FROM JUNE TO SEPTEMBER ON STEMS UP TO 30CM HIGH. AN EXCELLENT GROUND COVERING PLANT TO GROW AROUND THE POND, ITS CREEPING RHIZOMES FILLING IN ALL THE AVAILABLE SPACES AROUND LARGER PLANTS.

SMALL SCABIOUS — *Scabiosa columbaria*

THE NAME SCABIOUS COMES FROM THE FORMER HERBAL USE OF TREATING SKIN COMPLAINTS LIKE SCABIES. LIKES LIME RICH SOILS AND IS OFTEN, AND AS THE NAME SUGGESTS, SMALLER THAN FIELD SCABIOUS. MASSES OF PURPLE FLOWERS THAT ARE RICH IN NECTAR FOR BEES AND BUTTERFLIES. 30 CM.

SNAKE'S HEAD FRITILLARY — *Fritillaria meleagris*

A PERENNIAL BULB. THIS BEAUTIFUL PLANT HAS SINGLE PURPLE OR WHITE SPECKLED NODDING FLOWERS ON STEMS 20-40CM HIGH. IT IS NOW QUITE RARE IN THE WILD, DUE TO THE DECLINE OF ITS PREFERRED HABITAT OF DAMP MEADOWS, OFTEN BY RIVERS. THE FLOWERS PROVIDE AN EARLY SOURCE OF NECTAR AND POLLEN FOR BEES IN APRIL TO JUNE.

SWEET VIOLET — *Viola odorata*

SMALL, NO MORE THAN 15CM TALL. WILL THRIVE IN ANY NEUTRAL SOIL BUT PREFERS CALCAREOUS SOILS. PURPLE (OCCASIONALLY WHITE AND EVEN RED) FLOWERS APPEAR AT THE VERY EDGE OF WINTER IN FEBRUARY. SWEET VIOLET IS THE ONLY BRITISH VIOLET TO FEATURE THAT SPECIAL VIOLET SCENT, WHICH ATTRACTS THE FEW POLLINATING INSECTS THAT ARE AROUND SO EARLY IN THE SEASON. SWEET VIOLET IS A PREFERRED FOOD PLANT FOR FRITILLARY BUTTERFLIES AND MANY MOTHS - THE DECLINE OF VIOLETS IN THE WILD IS ONE REASON FOR THE DECLINE IN SOME OF THESE INSECTS.

SNEEZEWORT — *Achillea ptarmica*

A LOVER OF DAMP PLACES, THE WHITE, LONG-LASTING FLOWERS OF SNEEZEWORT ARE COMMON THROUGHOUT BRITAIN, THOUGH LESS SO IN THE SOUTH. PERENNIAL, HEIGHT TO 50CM.

SOFT RUSH — *Juncus effusus*

A TUFT FORMING RUSH 40-120CM IN HEIGHT. REDDISH BROWN FLOWERS TURN TO LONG LASTING YELLOW/BROWN SEED HEADS. THE SMOOTH GLOSSY UPRIGHT LEAVES FORM THE PERFECT SUPPORT FOR THE TRAILING STEMS OF GREATER BIRDS FOOT TREFOIL AND HEDGE BEDSTRAW. PERENNIAL.

TOADFLAX — *Linaria vulgais*

THE CLUSTERS OF CREAM AND YELLOW SNAP-DRAGON LIKE FLOWERS ARE PRODUCED WELL INTO THE AUTUMN MAKING TOADFLAX AN IMPORTANT PLANT FOR ALL WILDLIFE GARDENS AS IT PROVIDES A WELCOME SOURCE OF LATE NECTAR. PERENNIAL, TO 60CM.

Sweet Violet

Soft Rush

Sneezewort

Toadflax

St John's Wort

Water Forget-Me-Not

Water Avens

ST JOHN'S WORT — *Hypericum perforatum*

PERENNIAL. A PLANT OF OPEN GRASSLAND AND HEDGEROWS PRODUCING YELLOW FLOWERS FROM JULY TO SEPTEMBER ON STEMS UP TO 50CM IN HEIGHT, POPULAR WITH BEES AND HOVERFLIES. THE COMMON NAME IS DERIVED FROM ITS ASSOCIATION WITH ST JOHN THE BAPTIST AND 'WORT' MEANS HERB USED FOR TREATING WOUNDS. THE LEAVES ARE PERFORATED WITH TRANSPARENT DOTS OF OIL-PRODUCING CELLS.

WATER AVENS — *Geum rivale*

THESE DELICATE, NODDING FLOWERS CAN BE BLOOMING AS SOON AS APRIL. SEED HEADS ARE LONG LASTING. IDEAL FOR SHADY SPOTS. GROWS TO 60CM.

WATER FORGET-ME-NOT — *Myosotis scorpioides*

ANOTHER SUMMER LONG FLOWERING PERENNIAL FOR A DAMP SPOT, THIS ONE HAS TINY BLUE AND YELLOW FLOWERS. GROWS TO 45CM TALL. GROWS WELL BENEATH TALLER PLANTS AS IT IS QUITE SHADE TOLERANT AND CAN THRUST ITS FLOWERING STEMS UP THROUGH OVERLYING FOLIAGE.

WATER MINT — *Mentha aquatica*

PERENNIAL WITH LILAC OR PINK FLOWERS ON STEMS THAT REACH UP TO 40CM IN HEIGHT. GIVES OFF A VERY STRONG, MINT-SCENTED FRAGRANCE AND IS A RICH NECTAR SOURCE FOR BEES, BUTTERFLIES AND OTHER INSECTS SUCH AS HOVERFLIES. THE LEAVES TURN A RICH BRONZY-PURPLE IN AUTUMN.

WATER PLANTAIN — *Alisma plantago-aquatica*

PERENNIAL, GROWING IN THE MUD AT THE BOTTOM OF STILL OR SLOW MOVING PONDS. HANDSOME PLANTAIN-LIKE LEAVES GROW ABOVE THE SURFACE OF THE WATER WITH FLOWERING STEMS CLIMBING UP TO 90CM. PERFECT FOR DRAGONFLY NYMPHS TO CLIMB UP WHEN HATCHING! ITS SMALL BUT NUMEROUS THREE PETALLED FLOWERS OPEN ONLY IN THE AFTERNOONS.

WHITE CAMPION — *Silene alba*

THE WHITE FLOWERS, WHICH BLOOM FROM MAY TO AUGUST, ARE VISITED BY BEES DURING THE DAY BUT ARE AT THEIR MOST CONSPICUOUS AT DUSK WHEN THEIR SCENT ATTRACTS THE MOTHS THAT POLLINATE THE PLANT. MOTH CATERPILLARS EAT THE SEEDS INSIDE THE PODS. BIENNIAL OR SHORT-LIVED PERENNIAL, HEIGHT TO 80CM.

WILD BASIL — *Clinopodium vulgare*

PERENNIAL, HEIGHT 20 TO 40CM. OFTEN SURVIVES IN VERY DRY SOILS. PRODUCES NECTAR RICH PINK FLOWERS FROM JULY TO SEPTEMBER. ATTRACTS LOTS OF BEES.

Water Mint

White Campion

Water Plantain

Wild Basil

Wild Marjoram

Wild Thyme

Wild Strawberry

WILD MARJORAM *Origanum vulgare*

PERENNIAL, HEIGHT TO 40CM. PINK FLOWERS JULY TO SEPTEMBER ARE A RICH NECTAR SOURCE FOR BEES AND BUTTERFLIES. GROWS IN DRY PASTURES ON ANY NEUTRAL SOIL. ITS AROMATIC LEAVES CAN BE USED TO MAKE TEA OR BE ADDED TO TOMATO OR POTATO SALADS.

WILD STRAWBERRY *Fragaria vesca*

A PLANT OF DRY WOODLAND AND HEDGEROWS, SENDING OUT RUNNERS WHICH PRODUCE CARPETS OF WHITE FLOWERS AND RED FRUITS FROM APRIL TO JULY. THE FRUITS ARE SMALLER THAN GARDEN VARIETIES BUT HAVE SIGNIFICANTLY MORE TASTE. THE FRUIT IS ALSO LOVED, OF COURSE, BY MANY BIRDS. PERENNIAL.

WILD THYME *Thymus praecox*

PERENNIAL LOW GROWING (10CM) SHRUB. GROWS IN DRY AREAS OFTEN ON CALCAREOUS SOILS WHERE ANT HILLS WILL OFTEN BE COVERED IN WILD THYME. THE FLOWERS ATTRACT BEES IN PROFUSION. FAMOUSLY USED IN ALL SORTS OF COOKING IT'S ALSO A GOOD PLANT TO GROW AROUND PAVING, THE SPREADING STEMS ARE CRUSHED AND FILL THE AIR WITH THEIR SCENT!

WOOD ANEMONE *Anemone nemorosa*

PERENNIAL, NO MORE THAN 15CM IN HEIGHT. A PLANT OF WOODLANDS AND HEDGEROWS, OFTEN FORMING CARPETS OF WHITE FLOWERS TINGED WITH PINK OR PURPLE IN MARCH TO MAY. AN EARLY FOOD SOURCE FOR BEES, THIS PLANT IS IDEAL FOR PLANTING IN THE GARDEN IN SPRING BORDERS OR UNDER BROADLEAVED TREES AND SHRUBS. IT DIES DOWN DURING THE SUMMER AND TOLERATES DRY CONDITIONS. POISONOUS!

YARROW *Achillea millefolium*

YARROW'S FAMILIAR FEATHERY LEAVES GIVE IT THE NAME MILFOIL 'A THOUSAND LEAVES' DUE TO THE TINY SEGMENTS THAT EACH LEAF IS DIVIDED INTO. A FOOD PLANT FOR VARIOUS MOTHS AND A NECTAR PLANT FOR GREENFLY-DEVOURING HOVERFLIES. PERENNIAL, HEIGHT TO 40CM.

YELLOW FLAG IRIS *Iris pseudocorus*

ONE OF OUR STATELIEST AND MOST DISTINCTIVE WILDFLOWERS WITH ROBUST, BLADE-LIKE LEAVES. DESPITE PRODUCING YELLOW FLOWERS THE RHIZOMES YIELD A BLACK DYE. A MUST FOR EVERY WILDLIFE POND. PERENNIAL TO 1.2M TALL.

YELLOW LOOSESTRIFE *Lysimachia vulgaris*

AN ERECT PERENNIAL FROM THE PRIMROSE FAMILY, GROWING UP TO 1.5M TALL. SPREADS BY RHIZOMES INTO CLUMPS ON FENS, RIVER BANKS, PONDS AND LAKESIDES. YELLOW FLOWERS APPEAR IN JULY AND AUGUST. NOT RELATED TO PURPLE LOOSESTRIFE AT ALL.

Wood Anemone

Yellow Flag Iris

Yarrow

Yellow
Loosestrife

The Final Verdicts

Alison

I wasn't involved in the making of the garden as I started work at Wigglys the next year—it was very much in its early stages though. The plants in the gravel were tiny and it looked as though there would be huge gaps between them. The following year I was proved wrong! One of the areas I like the most is the meadow which looks stunning throughout the summer and even in the winter months when the seed heads are visible. I particularly love the *Verbena bonariensis* in the gravely patch, especially now that it has self-seeded, and the whitebeam tree is a fine example. Of the other plants in the garden, ragged robin is a particular favourite—it flowers and flowers forever. The ragged style petals look like they've been torn apart in a gale. Also I love the spindle, which is supplied in the Wiggly hedge packs. It has fantastic orange seeds encased with pink—such vivid colours. I like to walk around the garden now and again during my lunch breaks, especially on summer days, or to show the odd customer around. Plant identification is easy as the garden now has many of the species that we supply planted in it. I'd like to think that during the summer we could record the podcasts there, sitting amongst the wildflowers. I'm sure the microphones would pick up all the sounds of the birds and critters.

Over time I know the garden will mature. I'd like to see some taller shrubs to give the garden some height and honeysuckle scrambling over the walls would smell and look fabulous. I'd also love to underplant the hedge with wildflowers!

Jo

I joined Wiggly Wigglers after the garden was made, so I wasn't involved in its construction. I love the wildlife I see, especially the little robin that sits in the hole in the barn opposite my window, singing happily away to himself (or possibly to his mate). I also saw quite a spectacular sight one day—two swans flying past the window, like a pair of Concordes, en-route to the big pond in the farmyard. As a future development I think it would be great to have chickens in the garden.

Maggie

I use the garden to collect the hedging plants for packing and sending to customers. I'm particularly fond of the frogs, toads and newts in and around the pond. I would love to see a second pond.

Ricky

Sometimes I sneak off to the garden to get some herbs for cooking and sometimes I just pop round to have a look at all the flowers. And the wildlife! The dragonflies are just like helicopters buzzing around and the water boatmen on the pond remind me of my childhood. We should all take time out to go up to the garden, we are so lucky to have it close by; I always tell our customers to have a look around.

Jodie

I first came to Wiggly Wigglers in 1996. I had my own gardening business, and Heather wanted the garden tidy for when visitors came round.

The front garden had no character. There were flowerbeds around the walls, but these were overrun by weeds and couch grass, while a muddy path across the lawn was a short cut to the farmyard! The back garden, surrounded by a beautiful red-bricked wall, was mostly lawn, with a group of shrubs towards the back end and a few untrained raspberry canes in the far corner. There were several old pear trees dotted around the perimeter and an area of concrete next to the house. There was also an old rose border but it too was overrun with weeds and couch grass.

I used to visit for a morning about once a fortnight, mainly weeding out the tedious couch grass and bindweed, and generally making it look more like a garden. While weeding, I would often wonder what the garden may have looked like, years ago. Would there have been wonderful vegetable beds within the walled gardens, raspberry canes and fruit bushes, greenhouses full of exotic fruits and grape vines all grown to supply the main house? Also, would the front garden have had a gravelled path leading up to the front door, perhaps lined with a lavender hedge, with beautifully scented climbing and standard roses against the front of the house, which were picked to decorate and scent the rooms within?

The garden was maintained like this until, in 2002 we were expecting a royal visit. This gave us the impetus we needed to change the garden, and bring it back to life!

This wasted piece of ground was finally going to be revived, used and enjoyed not only by Heather, Phil and Monty, but also by the whole Wiggly Team and their families, and opened throughout the year to endless visitors.

The whole experience of this project was very exciting for me personally and I can honestly say I enjoyed every minute of it. We were pushed for time though, as Prince Charles was due at the beginning of May and it was also the busiest time in the Wiggly Calendar—spring !

It was just like 'Ground Force'! Heather was Alan, Pip was nicknamed Tommy, and I was Charlie! And of course we had to have a water feature! There were many helpers and even our families were hauled in to help finish the project. We worked late into the evenings and long weekends in amongst our Wiggly orders.

The garden was starting to take shape. One of my first jobs was to plant the native hedge, which gave the shape of the garden to work to. Heather, Phil and I then moved on to build the raised vegetable plots out of railway sleepers. This is when Phil found the baby mole, while Pip and Ronnie started excavating the pond. We

When finished, as you can imagine, the plants looked very small and the gravel stood out. Growth was needed to soften the edges and I was amazed how quickly the garden began to grow. Vegetables started appearing, flowers came out in bloom and the most beautiful wildflower meadow appeared as if from nowhere, filled with hundreds of poppies and oxeye daisies, just like the Cadbury's flake advert! Some of my favourite plants are the Rudbeckia which the bees just love… it flowers for so long. It's great to see our bird, bat and bug boxes being used and the pond is just buzzing with dragonflies, pond skaters and snails.

The garden is at it's best in July/August, although the dead seed heads of the flowers in the winter time, when there is a covering of hard frost, look amazing.

We feed the birds every week with a mixture of our seeds and mealworms. If you take a moment and stand in the back garden, you not only see and smell wonderful flowers, but you can hear the bees buzzing, frogs croaking and the birds singing. It can be almost overwhelming at times. I love meetings in the summer, because occasionally we get to sit in the hot tub and look at the garden. It makes all that hard work seem worthwhile.

that the Wiggly staff have gone on to do. I myself have taken ideas from this garden into my own garden, and I can honestly say, that I look at gardening very differently since I have been working in this one. You don't realise how important a garden is to wildlife and how to manage it, until you really get into how the different species of wildlife and flowers rely on each other, and the benefits they give to you as well as themselves. I no longer worry about the odd weed, or have my hedges trimmed neatly all year round. My friends and family might say 'You want to get on and cut your hedge, it looks a mess!' I have great delight showing them that there is a wren nesting in the hedge, and that there are mason bees using my bug boxes, which are pollinating my fruit trees, and the weeds are actually wild flowers which are not only beautiful, but beneficial to so many insects, birds and butterflies, which are controlling the aphids and slugs in my garden.

Wendy

I love all the wild-life in the garden (except the spiders!) and I particularly love the primroses and violets. The garden is a part of my work—I often go there to get hedge plants to pack up, and I also feed the birds. Unfortunately there's not enough time to use it as I would really like to—it would be lovely to sit out occasionally and watch the birds and other wildlife while relaxing.

Sylv

It's wonderful to see how the garden has been transformed into a haven for wildlife: all the lovely birds we have feeding in the garden, the butterflies and insects that live in amongst the wildflowers and grasses in the meadow. On a summer's day to see the insects on the pond, the birds swooping for a drink and just to sit and take it all in, is lovely.

> " *It was just like 'Ground Force'! Heather was Alan, Pip was nicknamed Tommy, and I was Charlie!* "

had done all the hard landscaping, paths, patio and pond, and even tractor driver Phil got to work with a shovel. Amazing! The hedge, orchard and specimen trees were all planted and so it was time for the exciting bits; sowing the wildflower meadow and planting up the pond.

We finished just in time, and it looked fit for a King! Sadly, Prince Charles only saw the front garden, as his visit didn't allow enough time for him to see the whole of the back garden. I like to think that he did look out of the dining room window though, and saw all our efforts. Of course he wasn't to know that we were running around like loonies for six weeks and that it was his visit that instigated the whole project!

The garden isn't quite finished in my eyes, but then the great thing about gardens is that you can keep adding things and taking out the things that you don't like. I would add a greenhouse (to me every garden needs a greenhouse) and I think a Victorian style one would look fantastic. This would prolong our harvest periods, and give us a chance to grow many more of our own seedlings. Some cold frames would also be good, plus some soft fruits like raspberries, strawberries and currants, and a few more seating areas for when we have open days.

This garden has given so many people so much enjoyment, and it is also a great experimentation ground for other gardens

Heather

As a family, or indeed as a business we never used to go out into the walled garden. It was pretty unpleasant and neglected. The patio area was broken concrete, just in front of that were a few rose bushes and then lawn with a few shrubs in the far corner. It was depressing with a dark, boring, sort of seventies feel to it.

There was no thought of developing a "family garden" for several reasons. The garden doesn't belong to us, it would have been too expensive for us as a family to justify and we wouldn't quite know where to start!

Once we had come up with the idea of The Wiggly Garden there were more and more reasons to develop it: it would teach us about natural gardening allowing our product base and knowledge to grow with the garden; it would be fun to make as a team; it would be great for our local wildlife; we would be making the most of our resources; it would provide a wonderful backdrop for catalogue photos; it could be used for meetings and open days and we could produce our own vegetables.

The plans were drawn up in November 2001 with a view to steadily building the garden throughout the next year. As it turned out we started the garden and then we were informed that Prince Charles wanted to visit to hold a tenants meeting at the farm. We decided that we should never have a better excuse than this one to get the garden sorted to some degree, so we embarked on a few weeks of serious "ground force". Several of us in the business helped during the week and outside office hours and several others from the village and community also gave up their time to help including: Pam (Pips wife), Ron (Pam's Dad), Pip himself, Margaret (Jodie's Mum) and Lee (Jodie's brother) and we begged and borrowed equipment from friends and relatives.

I remember we had lots of fun but it was really hard work. The sleepers for the veggie beds were recycled from Phil's grain store and we introduced thousands of lobworms to the orchard to help the soil, and in particular the drainage (which has worked really well by the way). We prepared everything and then Bridget who designed the plan and a colleague came one day, which happened to be raining like billy-oh, and planted up all the flowers, although we sowed the wildflowers.

My favourite animals in the garden are the worms, obviously. They are completely underrated in terms of what they do in the soil and how they make compost. Charles Darwin spent a long time studying worms and so if they were good enough for him…

Amongst the wildflowers teasel is really underrated, and I like snake's head fritillary and ragged robin. Best of all for me though is the overall effect of as many different species in the garden as possible. I like things 'en masse!'

In essence the fundamental aspects of the garden were completed in April 2002 and we enjoyed an afternoon entertaining Prince Charles with a tenants lunch and drinks. But what benefits we've seen since! There have been so many highlights!

We have all learnt so much from our own real garden that we won the Best in Show garden at Malvern. I personally have leant so much in terms of what attracts wildlife and how to look at plants in more detail to see their beauty, (unlike more garish tropical plants.)

So much has happened in the garden since we made it. We now feed over 15 kilos of seed every week. We compost nearly all Wiggly organic waste and our own (now the office uses a Bokashi bucket too which is fab).

And I have seen things I never would have noticed before—I saw a merlin in the field next door, as well as barn owls, little owls, deer coming down to the farm, and badgers playing in the newly planted meadow.

Not only is it a great garden but it was a fab community adventure, which continues every time the garden is "opened". Last time Rhian, Pam, Noelle and Rose (from the village and Wigglys) put on a tea for all of us once everyone had gone, and we ate it in the garden. Fab!

Sometime soon I'd like to see soft fruit in the garden (which is planned for this year) and I'd like to be able to dangle my feet in the pond without getting muddy (a tasteful bridge). One day a bit of shelter would be good (but I HATE those plastic conservatory things) and it would be great to have a greenhouse. And we are going to build a marsh this year around the boat which will be good.

One day I would love to hold a garden party on a balmy summer's evening with twinkly lights and candles and music and wine and chiffon dresses and nibbles. We'll see eh?

Monty (age 9)

I helped build the garden; in fact I have my own garden in the veggie patch and my own tree house. I helped make the pond—I pulled out the weeds before we sieved the soil to put on top of the liner.

When the dump truck wasn't on, I pretended to drive it.

Daddy found a mole in the front bucket of his digger and he picked it up and it bit him. I stroked it. It was all furry and its claws were really hard and it wiggled.

I like the wild area in the garden with the path and the benches best because it's colourful. Richard and me went pond dipping and we caught lots: newts, pond skaters and water boatmen.

I planted some cat grass in my veggie patch but Noah didn't like it. I grow carrots, potatoes, cucumbers and lettuce and cabbage and sunflowers.

I've got my own Can-O-Worms and I put left-overs in there and make compost. I took it onto *The Paul O'Grady Show* on the telly. And at the end of the garden I've got a tree house, a trampoline and an old boat that my uncle Billy gave me.

I use the garden to play in. Mummy and me slept in my tree house once.

I think its good to have bats. I know some people are scared of them but they wont hurt you.

I would like to change my vegetable patch by sowing my seeds in a pattern instead of planting them in rows, which can be boring.

I would like to see a swimming pool in the garden.

Our garden was just grass and a few pear trees before and now I think it's amazing!

Farmer Phil

Before, I regarded anything I couldn't mow as not of interest. Gardening meant weeding and grass had to be mown. When I was shown the plan, I was sceptical and felt that if it was to be restored, it should be to its 18th/19th century layout as a walled kitchen garden. I thought the pond would look too artificial and twee.

I got over-ruled and enjoyed helping to build garden—it was enjoyable to start from scratch rather than try to resurrect (and then fail) what was there.

My biggest scepticism was about the wild flower area which I was convinced would come up as a forest of docks and nettles—not only was I wrong, it is probably my favourite bit as it comes up a different colour each year and is very peaceful at the end of a day.

I love to relax in the garden, especially on sunny evenings.

In terms of wildlife, the garden has been a revelation. The increase in numbers and variety can be observed and the benefit spreads over a considerable area—at least one field in all directions. Everybody here is interested in the wildlife now, they ask questions and are inspired by information from the farm. Other people's interest has stimulated mine so that, when I see something, I bother to look it up and tell the story. For example I found a great crested newt in the farmyard then got everybody to look and take photos. Similarly the fallen tree in one of my fields created lots of interest. I've noticed birds that were probably here all the time but were unremarkable. Also people love to hear ongoing sightings of owls etc. and this relationship stimulates their interest in the farm animals as well. All this has greatly improved my understanding of the relationship between the environment and modern farming

methods which leads to the conclusion that with a little thought and effort, great benefits are achievable without affecting profitability, and it's enjoyable too. It has also shown that it promotes a far better attitude in me to do things because I want to, rather than being told to by DEFRA.

It pleases me that the variety of crops in our rotation promotes wildlife from insects upwards. The grass seed is great for all small mammals and therefore the predators like it too. It also helps minimise damage to worm populations, which have greatly improved our soil structure. By taking care not to harm bees etc. better pollination must be the benefit. Because we work alongside wildlife, we have to leave space for it—so hedges are maintained in a good network providing habitat for badgers to hunt—healthy badgers without TB will keep TB out, stressed badgers will promote it.

If we did it again, I might use different gravel or plant the gravel area more densely—in warm summer weather, the gravel gets very hot and fries some of the plants and it is a bit deep to walk on. In all though I love the garden. The pond turned out great and looks as if it's been there for ever—I really like the pond plants—the different colours and textures, flowers and foliage. I also like the hedge, which integrates Monty's bit with the rest—it means that the trampoline and Monty's other things are not much of a compromise because the hedge screens them from the rest of the garden.

Pip

I was involved in the construction of the Wiggly Garden right from the early stages doing the main groundwork, leveling, rotovating, digging the wildlife pond and laying the patio and gravel areas. The garden had once been a traditional walled garden but was now in a somewhat dilapidated state with expanses of concrete and grass.

The brief was to create a wildlife garden incorporating different environments to encourage a wide diversity of wildlife to set up home. The garden

should be able to quickly establish itself and integrate with the surrounding area as naturally as possible and also function as a working garden producing organic fruit and vegetables. This was not to be a "keep off the grass" garden! This was a garden to be used and enjoyed.

I found it very rewarding working on the Wiggly Garden project. It has proved that you can have a garden that is not only a fantastic habitat for many species of wildlife including butterflies (my favourite!) but also a functional kitchen garden and look good too.

We used locally sourced reclaimed materials such as flagstones and bricks; the cobblestones were very local as we found them lying around the farm itself (don't tell Farmer Phil!). This enhanced the look and the well thought out planting scheme produced a stunning result surprisingly quickly. The interest in the project locally also provided some enthusiastic volunteer support and so the garden evolved.

The garden has an ever-changing quality that is particularly pleasing. Not just from season to season but from morning to evening and rain to sunny.

The pond is a particular favorite of mine. I was very surprised to see how quickly after completion the pond was colonized. Frogs, water boatmen and all sorts of bugs and beetles soon appeared from seemingly nowhere. Like most kids I found the contents of ponds and streams fascinating and the pond dipping on open days is a brilliant way of educating the youngsters as well as being fun. Even the frequent visits of Toast the labrador for a cooling dip in the pond doesn't seem to deter the inhabitants!

The Open Days that are held in the garden are always enjoyable occasions. It's great to see so many people together, using and enjoying the garden and really bringing it to life!

As for the changes that I'd like to see; I think that the addition of some cold frames against the brick walls of the kitchen garden would add scope for increased variety of produce. Their design would have to take into account the presence of children and dogs and footballs though!

San

I wasn't employed by Wigglys at the time of the building of the garden although I used to help out when they were busy. I was about a lot during the evenings helping to catch up with the day-to-day operations, avoiding the need to get my hands too dirty! I told Heather constantly that they must be mad, and why would you pick the busiest time of the year to renovate a garden? Only later was I made aware of the urgency to sort the garden out in time for the royal visit.

It is hard to pick out my favourite part of the garden. If pushed I would have to go for the wildflower meadow. I love the way it alters with every season and the level of noise and buzzing you can hear while walking through it and the element of surprise as something flies by without warning. The overall flow of the garden works very well. I like the fact that you can walk right into it and can see all the products in action and the benefit they bring.

Looking at it from another point of view, it is fantastic to sit in the hot tub at night with a glass of champagne and listen out for movement in the garden. A great way to relax!

I don't have any real favourite creatures in the garden although it is nice to see new visitors each year. It is great to hear Heather getting excited about the different butterflies she has seen during the evening and it is good to see a different or uncommon bird visiting the bird tables. I do love the lavender walk way at the front of the house. It is a particular favourite of mine as it is fantastic for attracting the bees and it is a simple idea that can be easily replicated at home.

Seeing the birds feeding outside the office is a fantastic way to relax during a particularly stressful day. During the season of Open Days one task I had was to ensure the feeders were full—due to the level of feeding this task took upwards of 2 hours, and the birds had no problem getting through this. Now we rely on Phil the Gardener to fill the feeders every week to ensure they are never empty. We not only feed the birds in the garden but we have widened the feeding to include the area around the buildings as this is a natural extension to the garden. We have had a number of occasions of birds regularly visiting the despatch shed. This fascination has even spread to Phil the Farmer who has seen a family of swallows making a home in his workshop.

We have used the garden for many occasions. During the summer it is used a lot for our management meetings: one memory was in the wildflower area, we were all getting settled down to business and the bench that Rachel and I were sat on broke and there was this bundle of me and Rach on the grass! We moved back to the patio area and continued. On another occasion with the sun beating down on us, we had a meeting with our feet and legs dangling in the hot tub. It is lovely to have a nice oasis to retreat to for meetings; it also makes it more pleasant especially if we have an unpleasant topic to discuss. We have also held open days where we have used the garden as the focal point of the day, with a number of stations posted throughout the garden with staff to explain to the visitors what they are seeing and why they are seeing it. This has also involved the local community providing the tea party for guests and of course for us at the end of the day.

I find the garden really inspiring—it gives you the confidence to try something in your own garden. For example, I have planted a wildflower area at home, having seen how nice it can be and learning about the benefits it provides gave me the confidence to give it a go. I have numerous feeders around the garden with different seeds to attract different birds including three woodpeckers. I used to pick up all the apples and pears that fell to the ground in my own garden; now I am happy to leave them for the wildlife. All this is as a direct result of seeing what is happening in the Wiggly garden. If it has this impact on all its visitors imagine the level of benefit we could be providing for wildlife.

The best time of year for me is during the summer when the garden is a hive of activity. The flowers are in full bloom, the hedge has grown and thickened a bit more, the bugs, bees, butterflies and birds are all busy at work and increasing in numbers, the vegetable patch is so productive that all the staff now get to benefit from the crop as Heather has plenty of spare harvest. You can hear all sorts of chats in the staff room about how to best cook this or that.

In all I think the garden is a perfect working shop for our customers to see the products we offer and to get a true feel for what the product will achieve for them, which helps with the Wiggly ethos of traceabilty, practicality and durability. It also provides us with a perfect environment for testing products. Sometimes though, the housing units are not always used by the creatures they are for. For example last summer we saw a wasp's nest in both the sparrow parade and a birch tit box, but who cares? They were being used and all the creatures are providing benefits.

Not really being a "gardener" it is difficult to imagine ways in which the garden could be improved. As far as I am concerned it is working well and attracts a great variety of wildlife.

Richard

I wasn't involved in the creation of the garden given I've been in post with Wigglys for ten months. However we are in the process of creating a marsh area around Billy's old boat, which will add even more interest to the garden and give us the opportunity to introduce marshy species of plants like marsh marigold and cotton grass to attract an even greater array of invertebrates.

The garden is very much a tool for Wigglys to give visitors the chance to see how different natural gardening techniques can work in a relatively formal setting and how simple it can be to attract and support wildlife.

One of my favourite things in the garden are the bug boxes. To watch solitary bees plug hollow stems with mud whilst encapsulating an egg and bundle of pollen is a real treat. For me big red rose blooms are too obvious. I have always been more interested in the intricate relationship between our flora and fauna, and the Wiggly garden provides a diversity of habitats that support an array of natural activity.

I tend to use the garden as a means of showing visitors what is achievable and transferable to their own patch. In effect it is a working example of what we are about. I gaze into the garden when we do our Wiggly podcasts, and sometimes complicate the editing of the show with the occasional exclamation like 'sparrowhawk—on the beehive' or 'look at the goldfinches on the knapweed'.

We are running a series of courses and open days in 2006 which will see even more people enjoying the 'Wiggly Experience'. The garden lends itself to education by providing working examples of productive, natural gardening. Compost bins gush with nutrients, the pond positively exudes colour and animation, the meadow provides a waist height insect observatory, habitat boxes host a heap of beneficial fauna, raised beds provide the Wiggly Team with all sorts of goodies, and ancient fruit trees and ivy-coated walls conceal wrens nests and hunting hornets.

In many respects the essence of the Wiggly garden is its vibrancy. It both contributes to and reflects the success and creativity of the company.

Nicky

In the summer I love going to sit outside while eating my lunch with the warm summer sun shining down, the fresh air and all the different flowers/plants giving off their scent. The sound of the bees and insects buzzing around and the birds singing is amazing and I can watching them eating from the feeders, going to feed their young and hearing the loud tweeting of the babies in the nest boxes all wanting to be fed first! I find it relaxing and it is lovely to get out of the stuffy office with the ringing of telephones etc. I find it a time to recharge

my batteries and chill out...

There is one thing though I would really like to see in the garden to improve it—Chris Beardshaw! Now THAT would improve things no end!!!!! I will gladly give up any spare time to help that one come to pass!

Rachel

The change in the walled garden to me has been from 'Lower Blakemere Farm Back Lawn' to 'Wiggly Wigglers Wildlife Garden'. For me it started off as being a Tool to benefit the company, to be used to grow and develop Wigglys, but once established it turned into a haven for wildlife which was always around me but I had never studied or even seen it before.

I have enjoyed the bees most of all. I never could have believed that providing a few tubes in a box would attract nesting Red and Blue Mason Bees, I have regularly watched them go in and out the tubes to build their cells which house the eggs. I have then used these boxes to demonstrate the life cycle of the bee during open days and to my amazement—other people are on this learning curve too. Bumblebees have also enlightened me. The amount and varieties that have appeared in the garden after just a couple of years is amazing. I have never before studied one filling the pollen baskets on the sides of its legs to the extent that it can barely 'bumble away' back to the nest under the strain of weight they carry. At one point on a hot sunny day I poked one just to move it slightly for the ideal photograph. It did not take to this and immediately stopped collecting, bumbled up off the flower head dipping with the weight on its legs, as if to say, 'you have just disturbed a very busy bee!'

I have also enjoyed the colourful array of birds which seem to just pop in, such as the spotted woodpeckers. These are the type of bird which would not have been seen before and they have inspired me to put out feeders at my home, but typically with nature doing its own thing, they did not come!

The Wiggly garden is also a trial and error area. I personally trial new products for example, apple pumice, (which they don't seem to like). But I feel if a new product has been trialed here and really works, then it's a genuine product for the catalogue.

One of my interests in the garden is to take photographs, so hiding in a bedroom window or getting close up to the pond has been intriguing because I'm never quite sure what is going to turn up. Often I have gone out to photograph a bird but a much more interesting damselfly is out and about, but there is great frustration when it will not keeping still.

In general the garden benefits everyone. It was a very pleasurable day when I took a group from the local blind college around and they were able to point out the touch, feel and smell elements that were so important to them. The local community has attended open days and been amazed by the transformation, and most importantly all go home with ideas for their own wildlife heaven. All inspired by what they have seen in the Wiggly Garden.

Noelle

Working at Wiggly Wigglers is so different from a lifetime of hotel work. The change to working with worms is such a contrast! There is so much wildlife around now—it's a special treat when the birds come in to eat the mealworms from the tubbing machine while I work. I also really enjoy the podcasts and take them home to listen to with my husband Kevin.

Ann

The Wiggly Garden is somewhere we can go and relax if we have two minutes, which unfortunately isn't very often! The pond is a favourite area and in the winter I love being able to watch the birds feed on all the different feeders.

Index

Learn More...

Countryside Restoration Trust
www.livingcountryside.org.uk

A farming and conservation charity dedicated to restoring and protecting the countryside. The Trust demonstrates profitable farming which blends historic wisdom and sustainable modern methods to restore wildlife and maintain rural culture.

Eden Project
www.edenproject.com

Take a fresh look at the world and our place in it. The Eden Project promotes the understanding and responsible management of the vital relationship between plants, people and resources leading to a sustainable future for all.

English Nature
www.english-nature.org.uk

Working in partnership to conserve and enhance our landscapes and natural environment, to promote countryside access and recreation as well as public well-being, now and for future generations.

Garden Organic (HDRA)
www.gardenorganic.org.uk

Europe's largest organic gardening charity offers a wealth of expertise on how to grow fantastic vegetables, fruit and flowers in a sustainable way. This registered charity, formerly known as HDRA, has more than 31,000 members.

Herefordshire Nature Trust
www.wildlifetrust.org.uk/hereford

Herefordshire Nature is one of the 47 Wildlife Trusts that cover the country whose purpose is to make each county a place rich in wildlife for the benefit of everyone.

Linking Environment and Farming
www.leafuk.org

LEAF (Linking Environment and Farming) is the leading British farming and environmental charity working with farmers who care for the countryside to produce safe, affordable and healthy food.

LEAF is committed to a viable agriculture which is environmentally and socially responsible and ensures the continuity of supply of safe, affordable food while conserving and enhancing the fabric and wildlife of the British countryside for future generations.

The Centre for Alternative Technology
www.cat.org.uk

Europe's leading environmental centre offers information and resources to inspire, inform and enable you to lead a more sustainable lifestyle. CAT's display gardens have been cultured using organic methods for the last thirty years, and the Centre actively promotes composting and chemical-free pest control.